IS GENESIS HISTORY?

BIBLE STUDY
Leader & Student Materials

Thomas Purifoy Jr.
Director & Writer of *Is Genesis History?*

For use with the *Is Genesis History?* Bible Study Video Clips
Buy the DVD or download the HD video clips at IsGenesisHistory.com

Interior Layout by Five J's Design

Published by Compass Classroom,
605 W Iris Dr., Nashville TN 37204
www.CompassClassroom.com

Table of Contents

"For as were the days of Noah,
so will be the coming of the Son of Man."

—JESUS CHRIST (MATTHEW 24:37)

Introduction

This study explores what the Bible teaches concerning Creation, Adam and Eve, and the Flood.

It is intended to complement the film *Is Genesis History?* by looking at six key doctrines introduced in the first chapters of Genesis. These doctrines are related to the gospel and are important to understanding the nature of our salvation.

After all, Genesis records the foundational events in the history of the world. Jesus Himself was there at the beginning, forming everything according to His purpose. As the Apostle John tells us, *"All things were made through him, and without him was not any thing made that was made."* (John 1:3)

Genesis is therefore central to the work of Jesus Christ. Our hope is that by the end of this study you will better understand how the first chapters of Genesis are related to His plan of salvation.

Basic Study Principles

Throughout this study, we apply a series of basic study principles for understanding the Bible. Some may be familiar to you and others may be new. Please review these individually or as a class before starting the study.

1. **The Bible presents itself as an accurate, coherent book of history from beginning to end.** Although there may be different types of Biblical literature, they are all based on the bedrock of real events in actual time. For instance, both the book of Exodus and the Psalms refer to the actual crossing of the Red Sea by the Israelites, but they do so using different types of language in order to accomplish different things.

2. **Scripture should be used to interpret Scripture.** We can use one part of the Bible to understand another part. For example, Jesus, Stephen, and Paul all talk about Abraham at various times and ways. Their comments help us understand more about Abraham's history as recorded in Genesis. This principle of "Scripture interpreting Scripture" assists us in accurately interpreting the Bible.

3. **A doctrine is a statement summarizing the teaching of Biblical authors on a particular topic.** Since the Bible is the inspired word of God, even though there are many authors, it is possible to summarize what they jointly teach in a few statements. For example, all the different verses in the Bible about Jesus can be brought together to form a "doctrine of Christ," which includes statements such as "Jesus was fully God and fully man" and "Jesus atones for our sins." These exact doctrinal statements are not found in the Bible, but are useful summaries of what the Bible teaches.

4. **Doctrines are directly connected to specific events in history.** Just as branches grow out of the trunk of a tree, doctrines grow out of real events. Because Jesus was crucified and rose from the dead at a certain point in time, the "doctrine of salvation" teaches that "Jesus died for our sins on the cross and will one day raise us from the dead." If the first event did not happen, then the doctrine cannot be true.

5. **The Bible records events that are beyond our current experience.** Our finite understanding and knowledge should not be used to judge the historical accuracy of the Bible. For instance, had we been in Egypt to see the crossing of the Red Sea, we would have a better understanding of how the water acted under God's control. In the same way, if we were standing next to the tomb when Lazarus walked out, even if we could not understand *how* he was doing it, we could be sure he *was* doing it.

How to Use This Study

The *Is Genesis History?* Bible Study includes six lessons that can be used for group or personal study. Each lesson contains five parts: Setup, Video, Discussion, Differing Views, and Personal Study.

This study has been designed to "telescope" in length. If you want to teach it in a shorter timeframe, limit the number of questions asked. If you want to make it a longer session or even two sessions per lesson, you can ask more questions or go deeper into Differing Views.

Each lesson includes:

1. **Setup** — Ask a few questions to set up the current lesson.

2. **Video** — Watch the video clip that goes with the Lesson, then ask questions to discuss it. These are video clips of material not included in the feature film. Video clips are between 7 and 11 minutes in length.

3. **Discussion** — The teacher explains the background of the particular doctrine being discussed. A teacher may either review the material and teach it in his own words, or he may read the overview word-for-word. The class will then answer questions about three doctrinal statements supported by a passage of scripture. Answers are included in this book, so if you are teaching it to a class, students can keep their books closed for this section.

4. **Differing Views** — Discuss different views on these topics. We recognize there are a diversity of views on Genesis, so we try to explore some of the more important questions and topics.

5. **Personal Study** — Read through three passages of scripture and answer questions related to the doctrines discussed that week. This can be done at home by individuals or families.

FOR TEACHERS: Please make sure to watch the video and read through the lesson before class; there could be complex topics you will want to familiarize yourself with before the class.

Materials Needed

1. **Bible** — each participant should bring a Bible to class

2. **Bible Study Book** for each couple or person attending the class. (Leader and Student materials are both in this book.)

3. **Bible Study Video Clips** — If you do not yet have these videos, you can purchase them on DVD or digitally via download/streaming at IsGenesisHistory.com

Before You Begin

Everyone taking the class needs to do three things before starting the study:

1. **Watch the full film *Is Genesis History?*** Many of the topics discussed in the study assume the participants have seen the film. (Available at IsGenesisHistory.com)

2. **Read Genesis chapters 1–11.** It is important for everyone to have a refreshed familiarity with these chapters of Genesis.

3. **Pray** for the Holy Spirit's guidance and peace for everyone who is a part of the study.

Additional Reading

If you would like to consult additional books on this topic, the following titles are a good place to begin:

Creation and Change, Revised & Updated Edition, Douglas F. Kelly (Christian Focus Publications 2017)

Coming to Grips with Genesis: Biblical Authority and the Age of the Earth, Terry Mortenson and Thane Ury (Master Books 2008)

Creation in Six Days: A Defense of the Traditional Reading of Genesis One, James B. Jordan (Canon Press 1999)

1

Genesis as a Book of History
The Doctrine of Revelation

"One of the things that is very evident from the Genesis account is that it was intended to be understood as linear history."

— GEORGE GRANT

Read Proverbs 3:19

"The LORD by wisdom founded the earth; by understanding he established the heavens."

Ask Questions

- Why are questions concerning origins so controversial?

- If something is controversial, is that normally a sign of its importance? How important are the first chapters of Genesis to our lives today?

Watch Video 1 – "Genesis as History"

George Grant, PhD, Pastor

Ask Questions

- Why has the Christian church always understood Genesis to be real history?

- When did the church start to question whether Genesis was actually history, and why?

- If Genesis is history, how does what it records impact one's view of marriage? Of morality? Of one's relationship to God? What other areas of culture and the church does it impact?

- What do other writers of the Bible think about Genesis?

- Why is there such a strong push today to say that Genesis is not history?

NOTE: You can read this section to the class or review and summarize it.

The Doctrine of Revelation

The Bible is a book made up of different types of writing: history, laws, songs, prophecy, wisdom, and letters. One thing these writings have in common is their authors assumed they were writing about real people and events. As Peter explains:

"For we did not follow cleverly devised myths when we made known to you the power and coming of our Lord Jesus Christ, but we were eyewitnesses of his majesty. For when he received honor and glory from God the Father, and the voice was borne to him by the Majestic Glory, 'This is my beloved Son, with whom I am well pleased,' we ourselves heard this very voice borne from heaven, for we were with him on the holy mountain."
(2 Peter 1:16-18)

There are many internal indicators that Biblical writers were referring to actual events. The authors provide specific dates, identify locations, describe geographical features, or point out man-made monuments that were still existing when the original readers read the text.

Actual events such as the Exodus of the Israelites from Egypt, the giving of the Law to Moses, or the anointing of King David are the bedrock on which every type of Biblical writing is based.

In other words, the Bible is essentially a book of history.

Note that the word 'history' can be used in two related ways:

1. 'History' can refer to the written record of people and events in time (as in, 'the book of Kings is a history of Israel');

2. 'History' can be used in a more comprehensive sense to refer to the actual people and events themselves (as in, 'David's flight from Saul is history').

In this study, we will primarily use 'history' in the latter sense.

The Apostle Paul points out the connection between historical events and what the authors of the Bible reveal about those events when he tells the Corinthians: *"If Christ has not been raised, then our preaching is in vain and your faith is in vain. We are even found to be misrepresenting God, because we testified about God that he raised Christ, whom he did not raise if it is true that the dead are not raised."* (1 Corinthians 15:14-15)

Paul sees history as being directly connected to what he and the other apostles are revealing to people through their preaching. He explains that: *"The gospel that was preached by me is not man's gospel. For I did not receive it from any man, nor was I taught it, but I received it through a revelation of Jesus Christ."* (Galatians 1:11)

What is *revelation?*

Revelation is God's act of revealing Himself through His words and actions to people throughout the history of the world.

He has revealed Himself *generally* through the physical attributes of the creation itself. We see this in Psalm 19 where David says: *"The heavens declare the glory of God, and the sky above proclaims his handiwork. Day to day pours out speech, and night to night reveals knowledge."* This is known as **General Revelation.**

God has also revealed Himself through personal manifestations and spoken words. Psalm 19 continues: *"The law of the LORD is perfect, reviving the soul; the testimony of the LORD is sure, making wise the simple."* This kind of revelation is known as **Special Revelation.**

Special Revelation is the revelation that is included in the books of the Bible. It is what Paul was referring to when he talked about the revelation that God provided to him and the other apostles. It is also what Peter is referring to when he explains that *"no prophecy was ever produced by the will of man, but men spoke from God as they were carried along by the Holy Spirit."* (2 Peter 1:21)

Although General Revelation provides us enough knowledge to know that God exists, it does not provide a record of His words and deeds in time. This is why Special Revelation is so important: we cannot know what God has actually done in the past unless He specifically tells us.

There are three important points to the doctrine of revelation:

1

From the beginning of time, men and women were placed in the world so they could perceive God's power and divinity in the creation and worship Him.

Read Romans 1:18-20

"For the wrath of God is revealed from heaven against all ungodliness and unrighteousness of men, who by their unrighteousness suppress the truth. For what can be known about God is plain to them, because God has shown it to them. For his invisible attributes, namely, his eternal power and divine nature, have been clearly perceived, ever since the creation of the world, in the things that have been made. So they are without excuse."

What is the truth being suppressed by certain men?

The truth of General Revelation that God is powerful and divine, and should therefore be worshiped by everyone. Because this truth has been revealed through what God has made, those who reject it are without an excuse.

What is "plain to them," and how is it perceived?

God's invisible attributes are made visible through the creation, specifically His eternal power and divine nature. These can be seen by looking at the world around us, whether it is looking at a sunrise, seeing a mountain peak, watching the way a bird flies, or studying the complexity of DNA. Every aspect of creation reveals something about God.

What is the purpose of God revealing Himself through His creation?

He desires men and women everywhere to know Him and worship Him. In the verses immediately following this statement, Paul explains what happens to people who choose to worship the creation instead of the Creator: they eventually turn to sexual sin.

Why does Paul say God's attributes have been clearly perceived "ever since the creation of the world"?

He wants to show there has never been a time when man was not present on the earth to worship God. Paul is referring back to Genesis 1 and the creation of Adam and Eve on the sixth day of creation as the starting point for the worship of God.

Is there a connection between those who reject God's General Revelation and the desire to use intellectual disciplines (such as philosophy and science) to argue that He does not exist?

Yes, these are examples of different ways of suppressing the truth. People are turning to the creation to worship it instead of God. That worship can take many different manifestations, whether bowing down to an idol made of wood or an idol made of intellectual ideas. In the case of modern science, many people have taken the natural world and set it up as the maker of all things. Atheistic evolutionary theory is the idolatrous idea of the progressive self-creation of all things.

2 God spoke to select men who accurately recorded His words and actions, as well as the events surrounding them.

Read Exodus 24:3-4

Moses came and told the people all the words of the LORD and all the rules. And all the people answered with one voice and said, "All the words that the LORD has spoken we will do." And Moses wrote down all the words of the LORD.

Read Numbers 33:1-2

These are the stages of the people of Israel, when they went out of the land of Egypt by their companies under the leadership of Moses and Aaron. Moses wrote down their starting places, stage by stage, by command of the LORD.

Why is it important to God that His words and actions, as well as the events surrounding them, be recorded?

God reveals Himself through words and actions at specific places and times; they are a part of history. For instance, the Ten Commandments were spoken three months after the Israelites left Egypt. They are God's verbal commands intended to guide His people, so He instructed Moses to write them down for future generations to remember and follow. God also instructs Moses to write down the stages (or steps) of the people on their journey. He wants them to remember how He guided them, protected them, and provided for them at a certain time and place, so they can trust that He will do it again in the future.

How important is Special Revelation for knowing what God said and did in the past?

God's Special Revelation is the only way for us to know exactly what God has said and done in the past. When it comes to questions about origins, therefore, it is very important that we start with Special Revelation. As God's interactions with Moses on Mt. Sinai reveal, He was intentional about what He wanted Moses to write down. We must therefore be careful to base our understanding of history on what God has revealed to us about it.

Can General Revelation be used to know what God said or did in the past?

No, General Revelation is intended to reveal the invisible attributes of God such as His power and nature; it was not intended to reveal His words and deeds. In a sense, General Revelation is "ahistorical" since it occurs in the same way for all people at all times.

There are some people who say the Bible is "true" but that the events it describes are not actual history. Is there a problem thinking this way?

When talking about the death and resurrection of Jesus, Paul points out that if it did not actually happen, there is no hope for salvation. We all naturally understand that actions have consequences: if we don't fill up our car with gas, it will stop running; if we lock a door and lose the key, we cannot open it. Truth is therefore connected to reality: if something is said to have happened, but did not, then it cannot also be true.

3 God expects us to know the events recorded in the Bible and accept them as history so we can direct our lives according to what He has said and done.

Read Matthew 19:3-6

And Pharisees came up to [Jesus] and tested him by asking, "Is it lawful to divorce one's wife for any cause?" He answered, "Have you not read that he who created them from the beginning made them male and female, and said, 'Therefore a man shall leave his father and his mother and hold fast to his wife, and the two shall become one flesh'? So they are no longer two but one flesh. What therefore God has joined together, let not man separate."

Why does Jesus quote the account of the first marriage in Genesis 2 to address the Pharisees' question about divorce?

Jesus looks at the creation of the first man and woman—and their marriage in the garden—as the model for all other marriages. Adam and Eve were therefore the standard for all marriages coming after them.

Why is it important for Jesus' argument that the account in Genesis 2 be historically true?

Jesus is making the claim that what God did in the garden has direct consequences for all marriages after it. If the original marriage of Adam to Eve was not real, then it does not have authority over any other marriage. Jesus, however, points out there was an original structure to God's created order, and divorce was not part of it.

How important are a real Adam and Eve to the life and work of Jesus?

They are absolutely essential. Luke 3 shows that Jesus connects His lineage directly back to Adam as the first "son of God." The consequences of Adam's sin were the reason mankind and the world became corrupted and in need of salvation. Jesus came to earth to save us from the results of Adam's sin.

Closing Thoughts

The doctrine of revelation is the foundation of how we know who God is and what He has done in the world. Revelation, therefore, is where we must start when considering the question of origins. General Revelation reveals God's invisible attributes to the entire world, but it cannot tell us anything specific about history. It is therefore left to Special Revelation to reveal God's words and actions in time. Together, these two types of Revelation provide us an accurate, yet inexhaustible, fount of knowledge about creation and God Himself.

History, Science, and Authority

In the video clip, George Grant points out it was during the Enlightenment that a tension emerged between the authority of science and the authority of the Bible. The ground of struggle was whether the history recorded in the Bible or the history constructed by late 18th- and early 19th-century scientists was more authoritative.

That struggle for authority remains with us today. What is the proper relationship between history and science?

Dr. Grant explains that: "History is what helps shape and direct science itself, not the other way around. We need to understand *what* happened, and then science can help us understand *how* it happened."

Let's take a moment to look deeper at both history and science.

What is history?

Earlier, we said 'history' can be used in two related ways:

1. 'History' can refer to the written record of people and events in time (as in, 'the book of Kings is a history of Israel');

2. 'History' can be used in a more comprehensive sense to refer to the actual people and events *themselves* (as in, 'David's flight from Saul is history')

We regularly use both senses of history in our normal lives. In fact, our entire civilization is based on an understanding that the past contains real events that can be recorded and known today.

Just consider the importance of history to finance, healthcare, education, business, construction, politics, and the arts. Although people sometimes disagree as to what happened in the past (this is one of the reasons for the judicial system), no one disagrees that something actually happened.

What is science?

Just like history, 'science' can be used in two related ways:

1. 'Science' can refer to the process of studying the natural world in order to create a body of knowledge to help explain, predict, and control it.

2. 'Science' can refer to the body of knowledge *itself* that is used to describe the natural world.

Throughout the history of science, people have struggled with two basic problems: we are extremely limited in our human ability to study and understand the natural world; and the natural world is overwhelmingly complex.

In an attempt to overcome these problems, those pursuing science have always used "paradigms" or deductive frameworks to explain the data they discover. A paradigm could be compared to a pair of sunglasses used to see outside on a sunny day. Paradigms include sets of assumptions that help make sense of the immense amount of complex data—much of which cannot be identified, much less understood—throughout the world.

For instance, the paradigm of "plate tectonics" has helped geologists explain movements in the earth's crust. There are still observations and data, however, that the current paradigm of plate tectonics cannot explain. Nevertheless, it was considered a better paradigm than the view held until the 1960s, and will continue until it is replaced.

Unfortunately, paradigms can only alleviate the two problems, not solve them. When one looks at the history of scientific thought, it is clear that paradigms change and adjust over time as a result of new discoveries, new ideas, and new understandings. In many instances, the same data are seen differently from one generation to the next. The crust of the earth is a good example; clearly everyone could see it. One generation, however, thought it was static; another thought it moved.

Curiously, each contemporary generation thinks it has arrived at the most accurate views of the world. One can go back in history to see this. Yet even the most brilliant paradigms have been changed or replaced by following generations.

This has happened so many times throughout the history of science, it leads one to question the absolute authority of scientific statements. After all, if conclusions about the same data keep changing, how is it possible that scientists have arrived at the truth?

What are the different types of science?

There are at least three different types of science.

1. First, there is *operational* science, which performs experiments to explain and predict current and future events. Operational science is used in disciplines like chemistry, physics, or biology to try to describe the way the physical world or living organisms operate.

2. Next, there is *historical* science, which performs experiments and gathers evidence to make interpretations about what happened in the past. Historical science is used in disciplines like geology or paleontology to try to re-construct what happened in history.

3. There is another type of science called *applied* science. This is what we are most familiar with in terms of technology such as cell phones or medicine. Engineers and inventors often use observations about the natural world to create new things that rely on an understanding of how the world operates.

Most people are not aware of these distinctions, but usually lump everything together when talking about "science." This inevitably leads to confusion.

For instance, applied science has practical applications we can see and use, often based on the experimental findings of operational science. Historical science, on the other hand, cannot do experiments on what happened in the past; it can only do experiments in the present and examine pre-existing data to suggest explanations for rock formations and fossils.

Nevertheless, the authority of one type of science is often extended to other types of science. Just because we have cell phones does not mean every aspect of physics and chemistry believed today is accurate. In fact, although it may be surprising, the history of physics and chemistry is full of experimental ideas which "worked," which were accepted by brilliant men, and which have now been discarded.

This criticism applies even more strongly to the historical sciences, in which no experiments can be done on the past. Rather, evidence is gathered and fit into a historical paradigm. We should therefore be very careful about the authority of statements of historical science, especially those that reject the Bible as an authority.

Can science "tell" us anything?

Consider a phrase you may have heard: "Science tells us that…" with some observation or idea attached to the end.

'Science,' however, doesn't tell us anything. Rather, scientists who have particular views tell us things about the world that may be more or less accurate. To say "science tells us…" is to indulge in the poetic trope of 'personification.' After all, no has ever met Science and had a conversation with her.

One of the intentions of personifying science in this way is to make 'Science' more authoritative. This approach often comes up in discussions about origins, with some people granting to science an absolute authority it does not actually have. Science instead represents a variety of competing views of the world which change over time.

This is the reason science textbooks are constantly being updated. Scientific knowledge is not fixed, but is slowly shifting in one direction or another as paradigms change. It is not easy for the average person to see this since he is not privy to the latest scientific journals and debates. However, one need only pick up a science textbook that is 50, 100, or 150 years old, and it quickly becomes apparent how much things have changed in a relatively brief span of time.

This creates an additional problem for the authority of science. If science has changed as much as it has in the past century, how much more will it change in the next 50, 100, or 150 years? How many things that we are "absolutely sure we know" will be the laughingstock of future generations?

What is our ultimate authority in terms of natural history?

The question facing everyone in the modern world is this: is the Special Revelation in the Bible more authoritative than the consensus view of conventional scientists in terms of the natural history of the world?

This is why it is important to remember that science operates within paradigms to interpret data, that scientists are limited in their view of the world, and that scientific knowledge is constantly changing.

Although science can provide us with limited authority about the world, it can never provide absolute authority. This applies equally to conventional and creationist scientific ideas.

In other words, even the best creationist scientific model can only be an approximation of what actually happened. This is because science in itself can never provide absolute authority: it is always changing its views.

History, however, can provide absolute knowledge that is unchanging.

As a simple example, no one can change their biological history. We can all be sure we had parents, and our parents had parents, and so on back to Adam and Eve. Even if someone doesn't hold to the history recorded in Genesis, they would have to admit that genealogical links are more certain than scientific theories.

This is perhaps one of the reasons genealogies are used throughout the Bible to track the passage of time and show relationships between people. There is something fixed about biological father-son relationships that every culture innately understands.

As Christians, we are in possession of a document that presents itself as a complete history of the world from beginning to end. It is therefore important that we begin with that history when trying to understand the world through scientific means. Any other approach will inevitably lead to the suppression of that history.

Is creation (or nature) a book like the Bible that can be read by scientists?

Creation is not a book that can be read because it has no *words*. It is easy to know what a book is saying because it uses vocabulary and grammar. Creation, on the other hand, has trees, mountains, rabbits, and many more things that have no language associated with them.

Although there are scientists who like to think they are 'reading' some aspect of creation, they are mixing metaphors: a book with words is not the same as the non-verbal natural world. After all, how does one know what a tree or a mountain or a rabbit 'says' or 'means'? Without specific words to know the intentions of an author, any 'reading' becomes highly subjective.

Instead, scientists do experiments and make interpretations about the natural world in an attempt to understand it. Over time, a few of these interpretations are kept, but most are thrown out. Even if this is what scientists are referring to about 'reading' creation, it means creation must be nearly impossible to 'read' accurately since so many people are consistently mistaken about it. Again, this is because the metaphor is faulty: creation is not a book.

Nevertheless, this line of thinking remains popular today.

There is a desire for some to equate General Revelation with the creation itself, giving scientists the job of achieving a better understanding of General Revelation through scientific study. Since the "two books" of the Bible and creation must agree, then some are led to re-interpret Special Revelation through the latest "reading" of General Revelation. This was the thinking used in the early 19th century to merge views of deep time with the Bible, and then again in the late 19th century to merge evolutionary theory with the Bible.

Of course, the basic problem with this approach is that it has misunderstood how General Revelation actually works.

One does not need scientific knowledge to receive General Revelation. As David tell us in Psalm 19: *"The heavens declare the glory of God, and the sky above proclaims his handiwork. Day to day pours out speech, and night to night reveals knowledge. There is no speech, nor are there words, whose voice is not heard. Their voice goes out through all the earth, and their words to the end of the world."*

General Revelation can be seen and understood by everyone, regardless of their educational state or knowledge about the world. That is the point: it declares to everyone God's power and wisdom. Unlike Special Revelation, one cannot know more or less of General Revelation; one either recognizes it for what it is and worships God, or one suppress the truth of it.

Curiously, in the modern world, many of those who have greater knowledge of the creation actually reject General Revelation with greater vehemence. If General Revelation increased with scientific knowledge, then surely scientists would be the first to recognize God for who He is.

Clearly, creation is not a book to be read. Instead, General Revelation reveals the glory of God, His power, and His divine nature to all alike. Special Revelation reveals the specific words and actions of God in time. General Revelation can therefore tell us nothing about the actual history of the world; that role is left to Special Revelation.

From the beginning of time, men and women were placed in the world so they could perceive God's power and divinity in the creation and worship Him.

Read Acts 17:16-34

This is Paul's speech to the Athenian philosophers. Although the Athenians had only been exposed to General Revelation from what they saw in creation, notice how Paul introduces Special Revelation in terms his audience will understand.

Review the passage and answer the following questions:

- Where is Paul referring to things recorded in Genesis?

- Where is Paul referring to things recorded in the Gospels?

- How many statements about historical events is Paul making? Why are these important to his argument?

- What is the overall point Paul is making to the "religious" Athenians about their duty toward God?

- Why does Paul refer to Jesus' death and resurrection as an event that recently happened in order to encourage them to repentance?

There are many people in our culture today who are like the Athenians: they have been exposed to General Revelation, but have little knowledge of Special Revelation. As you speak to people you know, consider how you can use the events recorded in Biblical history as reasons for people to turn to God and repent before the next judgment occurs. It is possible you will receive the same response Paul did: some will mock you, but others will want to know more.

Pray that God would give you opportunities to speak the truth about His creation to others.

God spoke to select men who accurately recorded His words and actions, as well as the history surrounding them.

Read Jeremiah 1:1-19

This is God's call of Jeremiah to be His prophet. Jeremiah served God during the final years of the kingdom of Judah until it was destroyed by the Babylonians in 586 BC.

Review the passage and answer the following questions:

*   Jeremiah places his ministry within a very specific historical setting, in this case, the reigns of certain kings lasting from 626 BC to 586 BC. Why is this important?

*   God says that He consecrated Jeremiah before he was born. What does this tell us about God's plan to use people, their personalities, and their abilities in His service? What does that mean for you?

*   Why are God's words so powerful?

*   Why is it important to God that His words be taken seriously?

*   What is the connection God makes between what He is telling Jeremiah to say and what actually is going to happen in history?

*   What does this tell you about God's interest in the specific events of history, as well as His control over them?

We will look at God's control of history in the section on God's providence. For now, just remember that God chose certain men to accurately record what He was doing in history.

Pray that God would give you better understanding of what He has told us in the Bible.

God expects us to know the events recorded in the Bible and accept them as history so we can direct our lives according to what He has said and done.

Read Hebrews 11:1-16

This chapter is often known as the "Hall of Faith": it reveals the importance of faith behind key events and people in history. If you consider that these men are just normal people, you realize it was their faith in God's trustworthiness that gave them the ability to do what they did.

Review the passage and answer the following questions:

- Why are 'assurance and conviction' important aspects of faith? What does that mean in terms of being sure about something?

- Why are we to have assurance and conviction that the universe was created by the word of God?

- What was Abel sure of?

- What was Enoch commended for?

- What did Noah have a conviction about?

- What was the object of Abraham's faith?

- Why is it important that we understand the historical events surrounding these men and their decisions in terms of learning from them for our own lives?

- From God's perspective, how important is knowing history to our daily faith?

Just because we cannot see something at this moment does not mean our conviction and assurance of it is not reasonable. History reminds us that God has acted in space and time in important ways, and that He is still doing so today.

Pray that God would give you faith to trust Him in whatever circumstance you find yourself.

2

The First
Seven Days
The Doctrine of Creation

*"To me, six day creation is totally compatible with
what a designer would expect."*

— STUART BURGESS

Read Genesis 1

In the beginning, God created the heavens and the earth. The earth was without form and void, and darkness was over the face of the deep. And the Spirit of God was hovering over the face of the waters.

And God said, "Let there be light," and there was light. And God saw that the light was good. And God separated the light from the darkness. God called the light Day, and the darkness he called Night. And there was evening and there was morning, the first day.

And God said, "Let there be an expanse in the midst of the waters, and let it separate the waters from the waters." And God made the expanse and separated the waters that were under the expanse from the waters that were above the expanse. And it was so. And God called the expanse Heaven. And there was evening and there was morning, the second day.

And God said, "Let the waters under the heavens be gathered together into one place, and let the dry land appear." And it was so. God called the dry land Earth, and the waters that were gathered together he called Seas. And God saw that it was good.

And God said, "Let the earth sprout vegetation, plants yielding seed, and fruit trees bearing fruit in which is their seed, each according to its kind, on the earth." And it was so. The earth brought forth vegetation, plants yielding seed according to their own kinds, and trees bearing fruit in which is their seed, each according to its kind. And God saw that it was good. And there was evening and there was morning, the third day.

And God said, "Let there be lights in the expanse of the heavens to separate the day from the night. And let them be for signs and for seasons, and for days and years, and let them be lights in the expanse of the heavens to give light upon the earth." And it was so. And God made the two great lights—the greater light to rule the day and the lesser light to rule the night—and the stars. And God set them in the expanse of the heavens to give light on the earth, to rule over the day and over the night, and to separate the light from the darkness. And God saw that it was good. And there was evening and there was morning, the fourth day.

Ask Questions

- When you look at Genesis chapter 1, what are some of the things you notice about it as a record of events?

- How many different time indicators are there? *evening, morning* *first day, second day etc.*

Watch Video 2 – "The Nature of Creation"

Stuart Burgess, PhD, Mechanical Engineer

Ask Questions

- Dr. Burgess speaks of the world as being designed from an engineer's perspective. How does this change your way of thinking about creation?

- Why, from a design perspective, is it important that creation happen in a short period of time (i.e., six days)?

- Although water and air are common things, Dr. Burgess talks about them being impressively designed. What does that tell us about the way God provides for us in every aspect of our lives?

- How important is it to accept what the Bible says about the creation of the world? *God's Word is all true, not partially*

The Doctrine of Creation

The creation of the heavens and the earth is recorded in the first chapter of Genesis. Throughout the rest of the Bible, the authors refer back to creation as the beginning of everything, including time.

What is the doctrine of *creation?*

The doctrine of creation refers to God's act of creating the heavens and the earth out of nothing, then forming everything that exists in the span of six days.

The doctrine of creation reveals some important aspects about God.

First, we see that God is *transcendent.* This means He is outside time and space, and far beyond us. And yet, at the same time, we see that God is *immanent.* This means He is also involved with His creation shaping it, designing it, and engaging it. We see Him talking to man and woman on a personal level.

The doctrine of creation includes the absolute power or *omnipotence* of God. His ability to create simply by speaking things into existence is an act of unlimited power.

God also has complete *freedom* in creating; no one required Him to create the world the way He created it, when He created it, or in the order He created it.

Finally, the doctrine of creation is directly related to the doctrine of revelation. God designed the world so that He could be perceived in it. He created people who could perceive both General and Special Revelation. Then He spoke to them directly so that they would know who He is and what He has done, ultimately leading to worship.

What do other authors in the Bible say about creation?

1 God created the universe out of nothing by the power of His word; this reveals His transcendent power. Nevertheless, He created everything for men and women to be able to walk with Him and know Him; this reveals His immanent presence.

Read Hebrews 11:1-8, 13-16

Now faith is the assurance of things hoped for, the conviction of things not seen. For by it the people of old received their commendation. By faith we understand that the universe was created by the word of God, so that what is seen was not made out of things that are visible.

By faith Abel offered to God a more acceptable sacrifice than Cain, through which he was commended as righteous, God commending him by accepting his gifts. And through his faith, though he died, he still speaks. By faith Enoch was taken up so that he should not see death, and he was not found, because God had taken him. Now before he was taken he was commended as having pleased God. And without faith it is impossible to please him, for whoever would draw near to God must believe that he exists and that he rewards those who seek him.

By faith Noah, being warned by God concerning events as yet unseen, in reverent fear constructed an ark for the saving of his household. By this he condemned the world and became an heir of the righteousness that comes by faith. By faith Abraham obeyed when he was called to go out to a place that he was to receive as an inheritance. And he went out, not knowing where he was going...

These all died in faith, not having received the things promised, but having seen them and greeted them from afar, and having acknowledged that they were strangers and exiles on the earth. For people who speak thus make it clear that they are seeking a homeland. If they had been thinking of that land from which they had gone out, they would have had opportunity to return. But as it is, they desire a better country, that is, a heavenly one. Therefore God is not ashamed to be called their God, for he has prepared for them a city.

Why is faith important to understanding creation?

Faith is trusting that God's word is powerful, and that what He has told us is accurate.

How is a faith based on accepting the reality of God's actions in history different from blind faith?

The power of faith does not come from inside a person, but from the dependability and power of the person being trusted. Blind faith often refers to an irrational trust of someone who cannot do what is expected of them. The author of Hebrews, however, presents a long list of people who trusted God would do what He said He would do, and were vindicated for it.

Some people have said that God created the universe out of pre-existing materials. Does this passage speak to that question?

The author tells us that God made the world just using His words, bringing everything into existence from nothing. During the time the author of Hebrews was writing, there were different ideas about creation, including the idea that the gods made the world out of things that already existed. He is therefore speaking directly against this idea in this passage.

What do these verses tell us about the relationship between faith and God's power?

Anyone who can create everything out of nothing has absolute power. He can therefore be absolutely trusted.

Why does the author mention all these different men from the first chapters of Genesis? Would it make any difference to the author's argument if the people and events he is listing were not real?

These men are examples of people staying faithful to God and His word in extremely difficult circumstances. If they did not actually live and do what the author says they did, it would make an enormous difference. The author wants his readers to know that if God related this way in the past to people who had faith in Him, He will do the same in the present.

Why does the doctrine of creation always need to rely on the miraculous acts of God?

Creation is something far beyond our experience and comprehension. As Dr. Burgess explains, even the things we take for granted are much more complex than we realize. Furthermore, God's act of creating was a way of revealing Himself. Whenever God reveals Himself, there is some miraculous aspect to it beyond our comprehension. This is why Paul compares receiving the knowledge of Christ to God's first act of creation: *"For God, who said, 'Let light shine out of darkness,' has shone in our hearts to give the light of the knowledge of the glory of God in the face of Jesus Christ."* (2 Corinthians 4:6)

2 God created everything in six normal days to provide a structure of time for man to live by. In other words, time was made for man, not man for time.

Read Exodus 20:8-11

"Remember the Sabbath day, to keep it holy. Six days you shall labor, and do all your work, but the seventh day is a Sabbath to the LORD your God. On it you shall not do any work, you, or your son, or your daughter, your male servant, or your female servant, or your livestock, or the sojourner who is within your gates. For in six days the LORD made heaven and earth, the sea, and all that is in them, and rested on the seventh day. Therefore the LORD blessed the Sabbath day and made it holy."

This is the fourth commandment God gave Moses on Mt. Sinai. Why is this an important verse for understanding the duration of time in which creation happened?

God is revealing to the Israelites that His command about work and rest for a normal week is patterned on His own schedule of work and rest during the first seven days of creation.

If God is all-powerful, He could have created the world and rested in any amount of time. Why does He make a connection between the creation week and seven days?

God chose to create and rest in seven normal days to provide us the model for our weekly cycle. He even created mornings and evenings on the days before there was a sun and moon to show that these are essential structures for measuring time which He built into the creation. After all, it would seem no less strange to an Israelite than it does to us to have a source of light, and mornings and evenings, without the sun. Yet God chose to create this way for a purpose: He is the ultimate source of light for the world. God reveals the basic connection between our weekly cycle and the creation week in the fourth commandment.

How was God providing us a pattern of work and rest in our own lives? Why is this an important pattern for us to follow?

Just as God designed the eye to see light, and the body to digest food, He designed our ability to work and rest to fit into specific cycles that are good for us. If we do not pursue work and rest throughout the week, then we will be unhealthy; if we work seven days and do not rest, we will also be unhealthy. During the French Revolution, the government attempted to change the week to 10 days; it was an utter failure and they had to return to a normal seven day cycle of work and rest.

It is interesting to note that most major divisions of time are based on astronomical cycles (the day, the month, and the year), but the seven-day week is not based on anything we can observe. Instead, the week goes back to the very first week of creation. We therefore have a constant reminder that God structured the creation of the entire universe on a pattern designed for our well-being: six days of work and one of rest.

Read Mark 2:27-28

One Sabbath [Jesus] was going through the grainfields, and as they made their way, his disciples began to pluck heads of grain. And the Pharisees were saying to him, "Look, why are they doing what is not lawful on the Sabbath?"... And [Jesus] said to them, "The Sabbath was made for man, not man for the Sabbath. So the Son of Man is lord even of the Sabbath."

What does this tell us about the purpose of the days of the week?

The days of the week were designed for us. God created those time cycles and worked within them to provide us a chronological structure for our lives.

What point in time is Jesus referring back to when He says "The Sabbath was made for man?"

Jesus is referring back to the seventh day of the creation week in Genesis 2:2-3. Moses tells us that *"God blessed the seventh day and made it holy."*

What does Moses mean when he says in Psalm 90:2-4: *"Before the mountains were brought forth, or ever you had formed the earth and the world, from everlasting to everlasting you are God. You return man to dust and say, 'Return, O children of man!' For a thousand years in your sight are but as yesterday when it is past, or as a watch in the night."*

Sometimes people talk about "God's time" as being a long age, but that is inaccurate: God is not bound by time.

In other words, to man a thousand years is always a thousand years and a day is always a day, but to God, who stands outside of time, they are the same. This means that when normal time indicators are given in the Bible, they are intended to communicate the timescale we all experience.

God made time for man to live within; it something uniquely designed for us. Although God and angelic beings live outside of time, they can interact within time.

At some point, however, God takes man out of time to be with Him. This is what we see in Genesis 5: *"When Enoch had lived 65 years, he fathered Methuselah. Enoch walked with God after he fathered Methuselah 300 years and had other sons and daughters. Thus all the days of Enoch were 365 years. Enoch walked with God, and he was not, for God took him."*

Why is time so important in Scripture?

Because God reveals Himself to man in time. This is the very strong connection between the doctrine of creation and the doctrine of revelation.

3 God's original creation was "very good" and operated on a different set of relationships than we currently experience. In His goodness, God provided Adam and Eve everything they would need to know and worship Him.

Read Genesis 1:28-2:4

And God said, "Behold, I have given you every plant yielding seed that is on the face of all the earth, and every tree with seed in its fruit. You shall have them for food. And to every beast of the earth and to every bird of the heavens and to everything that creeps on the earth, everything that has the breath of life, I have given every green plant for food."

And it was so. And God saw everything that he had made, and behold, it was very good. And there was evening and there was morning, the sixth day.

Thus the heavens and the earth were finished, and all the host of them. And on the seventh day God finished his work that he had done, and he rested on the seventh day from all his work that he had done. So God blessed the seventh day and made it holy, because on it God rested from all his work that he had done in creation.

What do these verses tell us about the nature and purpose of God's original creation?

God's original creation was very good. It was created not only for our benefit and use, but for the benefit of living creatures.

If, in the original creation, mankind and animals were only to eat plants, what does that point to?

It points to a world very different from ours, one without carnivory and animal death. As Dr. Kurt Wise points out in *Is Genesis History?*, this is somehow a world without natural evil. We cannot understand from a physical perspective how this could have been because we are on the other side of the Fall of mankind (something we will discuss in another lesson).

Nevertheless, we are given a hint of this unfallen world—and a hint of the new heavens and new earth that we look forward to—when God tells the prophet Isaiah: *"The wolf shall dwell with the lamb, and the leopard shall lie down with the young goat, and the calf and the lion and the fattened calf together; and a little child shall lead them. The cow and the bear shall graze; their young shall lie down together; and the lion shall eat straw like the ox. The nursing child shall play over the hole of the cobra, and the weaned child shall put his hand on the adder's den. They shall not hurt or destroy in all my holy mountain; for the earth shall be full of the knowledge of the LORD as the waters cover the sea."* (Isaiah 11:6-9)

Was the seventh day also a normal day?

Yes, the seventh day was also a normal day. This is in line with Moses' comments in Exodus 20 and Jesus' comments in Mark 2. The idea of God's rest, however, is associated with the heavenly rest that believers have in store for them. This is what the author of Hebrews is referring to in chapter 4. Some have suggested that the seventh day is different from the other days in terms of duration, but there is nothing anywhere in the Bible to suggest that. Rather, the seventh day is a normal day set apart because God made it special.

Closing Thoughts

If God were not so interested in time, He would not have talked about it so much in His word. The fact that He has, however, should make us take note of what He says about it and what our response to it should be. There is no better way to end a discussion of time than with the prayer of Moses to God: *"For all our days pass away under your wrath; we bring our years to an end like a sigh. The years of our life are seventy, or even by reason of strength eighty; yet their span is but toil and trouble; they are soon gone, and we fly away. Who considers the power of your anger, and your wrath according to the fear of you? So teach us to number our days that we may get a heart of wisdom."* (Psalm 90:9-11)

Non-Literal Interpretations of Genesis

There are some Christians who do not think Genesis 1 and 2 should be taken as a literal record of sequential historical days. Instead, they interpret the days and events of the first chapters of the Bible in a variety of ways, such as a 'literary framework,' 'God's workdays,' or as a 'functional cosmic temple.'

There are useful observations in all these approaches. Aspects of them, in fact, can be found throughout the history of the church's interpretation of Genesis. Ancient, medieval, and early modern commentators noticed the parallel literary pattern of three days of forming and three days of filling, or that God acts like a workman in creating the earth, or that the garden of Eden has many similarities to the structure of the tabernacle and temple.

They saw these patterns as quite intentional. The metaphor of a master builder was used for God who, like the architects of the mighty cathedrals, intricately designed real structures to communicate theological truths. They knew God told Moses in Exodus 25:40 to build the tabernacle *"after the pattern…which is being shown you on the mountain."* They also knew the author of Hebrews goes on to explain that this real structure was just *"a copy and shadow of the heavenly things."* (Hebrews 8:5) They understood that God expected us to notice these patterns and figure out what they meant.

This intentionality is why there is so much similarity between Eden, the tabernacle, and "the heavenly things": they were all designed by the same Designer to be His dwelling place with man. These sorts of connections between reality and theology were obvious to the commentators; when they read the Bible, they saw that God put patterns everywhere He revealed Himself.

Can history be both literal and symbolic?

What makes these patterns so fascinating is that they are actually embedded in real history. There are patterns and symbols throughout the Bible, from the life of Moses to the life of David to the life of Jesus, all of which are equally literal *and* symbolic. If God is both transcendent and immanent— and far beyond us in creativity— we should expect that there are numberless things built into the creation and its history that uniquely reveal His delight in patterns as ways to understand Him better.

This is important to note: most commentators throughout the history of the church have understood that, for these patterns to have theological meaning, they had to be historically real. It was not until the era of modern philosophy that a whole discipline of theological thinking arose which separated theology from history. There began to be a view that if something has a pattern, it was structured that way by a later author and was likely not a reflection of real events.

This thinking seems to have influenced contemporary interpretations of the first chapters of Genesis. Many interpreters see the obvious patterns in the days of creation, and therefore separate those patterns from real history. Whether the pattern is a literary structure, a relationship to workdays, or an image of the temple, commentators assert that the purpose of the early chapters of Genesis is to teach theology rather than history. As a result, these interpretations de-historicize various sections of Genesis.

This creates three basic problems.

First, modern interpreters do not replace the record in Genesis with another history; they simply say it isn't history. But if Genesis isn't a literal record of events, then what actually happened at the beginning? Considering that the role of Special Revelation is to provide us an accurate record of the words and actions of God in time, it seems strange that the first chapters of that revelation would not do the very thing one would expect it to do: tell us how God created the world and everything in it.

Curiously, this is where modern commentators say they are not scientists and point to the conventional scientific community to provide that history. Although these interpreters would not do this with any other part of the Bible, they do it with Genesis 1 and 2. Leaving aside the question as to whether contemporary scientists are qualified to speak authoritatively on matters of history, the result is that these interpretations are used to justify replacing the Biblical timeline of creation in six days with the conventional timeline of universal formation over billions of years.

Second, modern commentators do not provide any clear consensus as to where to draw the line between what is only theological and what is theological-historical. In other words, where does real history begin?

There is much discussion of "genre" as being the determining factor, but it quickly becomes subjective as to where one draws the historical line. Considering this is not a problem anywhere else in Genesis (much less the other historical books of the Bible), it leads one to believe that there is not a real distinction here either, and that the earlier commentators were right: Genesis is both literal and symbolic.

Third, the witness of other inspired authors creates a significant problem for modern interpretations that seek to separate the theological and the historical. Shouldn't we rely on the interpretations of men like Jesus, Paul, and Peter for understanding what the text actually means?

Even in the Old Testament, the prophet Isaiah provides more than sufficient evidence that the theology and history of Genesis are inseparably joined. He quotes God Himself saying that the doctrine of creation is the primary reason He can be trusted in all matters, including His control of world events.

It is obvious that Biblical authors were familiar with the text of Genesis and saw how it connects to the real world. This is why their views must come prior to recent attempts at re-interpretation through the discovery of Ancient Near Eastern texts such as the Gilgamesh epic, Enuma Elish, or others. If anything, these texts are confirmation that the ancient pagan world retained something of its memory of the global flood and the world before it.

When, however, one looks at the Biblical text in comparison with these pagan documents, the differences are significant. From the transcendence of God, to the consequences of moral choices for the created order, to the realistic presentation of people and events, there are an overwhelming number of indicators, both within the early chapters and within other parts of the Bible, that Genesis is a literal account of history. This is the perspective of Jesus and His disciples.

Why Should Genesis 1 be considered History?

Besides what has already been said, here are a number of additional reasons why Genesis 1 should be seen as literal history formed by God with symbolic intent:

1. **The use of the Hebrew word 'day' (yom) modified by the cardinal numbers 'one,' 'two,' 'three,' 'four,' 'five,' and 'six,' alongside the nouns 'morning' and 'evening' are all specific time indicators referring to a normal week.** This is the common vocabulary we see in ancient times, medieval times, and modern times. Wherever these words are used in other parts of the Pentateuch or other historical narratives of the Bible, we interpret them as referring to normal time. In fact, the Hebrews who translated Genesis into Greek for the Septuagint in the 2nd century BC used the normal Greek word for a 24-hour day in Genesis 1, even though there were other Greek words that signified a long period of time.

2. **Although there are a handful of instances of 'day' being used in non-literal ways in the Old Testament, it is clear from usage and context these are not the case in Genesis 1.** Theologian Geerhardus Vos explains, "It is not accurate to say that the days are God's days. God *ad intra* does not have days. Creation is an act proceeding outwardly from God.... Appealing to the eternal Sabbath is also of no avail. Although God's Sabbath is certainly endless, that cannot be said of the first Sabbath.... The use of the term 'day' in Genesis 2:4 is figurative, but in Genesis 1 figurative language is not used. What one must show is another place in Scripture where a first, a second, a third day, etc., are just as sharply separated and and nevertheless describe periods of time. The 'day of the Lord' of the prophets refers to a specific day—that is, a day on which the Lord appears for judgment, even though His judgment may last longer than one day."[1]

3. **There are numerous statements in Exodus that compare the duration of God's creation to something already familiar to the enslaved Hebrews: one week of seven days.** The most well-known of these is integral to the Fourth Commandment.

4. **Genesis provides what one would expect at the beginning of a universal history: a record of what actually happened *in the beginning*.** Often, the 'superiority of the present' is invoked to say the Israelites

---

1   Geerhardus Vos, *Reformed Dogmatics* (Lexham Press, 2014), 169.

were a primitive people who could not understand what actually happened; but this is pure speculation that runs counter to the witness of the rest of the Bible. The observation that God provided an account so different in structure and content from other literature in the Ancient Near East is testimony that He gave them the one accurate account, especially considering they were surrounded by Egyptian creation stories. He certainly wasn't waiting 3500 years for a handful of scientists in the mid-20th century finally to explain what He did in the beginning.

5. **Genesis 1 and 2 are narrative history, as can be seen in the way events flow from one to another through chapter 3 and forward.** Again, Vos explains, "within the narrative of Scripture, the creation narrative is interwoven like a link in the chain of God's saving acts. God does not make a chain of solid gold, in which the first link is a floral wreath. If the creation history is an allegory, then the narrative concerning the fall and everything further that follows can also be allegory. The writer of the Pentateuch presents his work entirely as history."[2] Any attempt to find additional time between the morning/evening/day repetition, or to see the days as a list of highlights over a long period, or to call it poetry, is a rejection of basic linguistic aspects of the text.

6. **Dr. Steve Boyd's statistical analysis of the Hebrew verbs used in Genesis 1:1-2:4 in comparison with other narrative passages of the Old Testament reveals a "99.5% confidence level" that the passage is narrative history.** As he explains, "the weight of evidence is so overwhelming that we must acknowledge that Biblical authors believed that they were recounting real events. We must therefore call their work history."[3]

7. **There is a significant "numerical harmony" based on the numbers** *three* **and** *seven* **in Genesis 1:1-2:4.** Rabbinic scholar Umberto Cassuto observes that:[4]

---

2   Ibid., 161.

3   Steven W. Boyd, *Radioisotopes and the Age of the Earth* (Institute for Creation Research, 2000), 690.

4   Umberto Cassuto, *From Adam to Noah* (The Magnes Press, 1972), 13-15.

- The entire section is divided into seven paragraphs, one per day.

- The nouns *God, heaven,* and *earth* are repeated in multiples of seven throughout the passage: *God* 35 times, *heaven* 21 times, and *earth* 21 times.

- *Light* and *day* are each mentioned seven times in the first paragraph. *Light* is mentioned seven times in the fourth paragraph.

- *Water* is mentioned seven times in paragraphs two and three together.

- *Beasts* is mentioned seven times in paragraphs five and six together.

- The expression *it was good* appears seven times.

- The first verse has seven words; the second verse contains fourteen words; and the seventh paragraph has three sentences, each of which contains seven words and has the expression *the seventh day* in the middle.

Cassuto finishes his overview with the final observation, "to suppose all of this is a mere coincidence is not possible."

8. **James Jordan identifies numerous chisastic structures in the first chapter of Genesis.** Chiasm is a literary structure based on the Greek letter *chi* (X). This structure basically follows a pattern that inverts itself as it describes a flow of events, such as A,B,C,D,C',B',A' with D being in the center. Jordan observes numerous chiastic structures within the passage, from the days of creation, to what is being created, to what is being signified.[5] Chiasms linked to history can be found throughout the rest of the Bible, too, as Gordon Wenham has observed with the flood account and Kenneth Bailey with a large section of Luke. Such consistent patterns in historical narratives are additional evidence that God was ordering events according to His own purposes.

In light of all these points, how is it possible that some modern interpreters want to deny that Genesis 1 is literal history?

---

5   James B Jordan, *Creation in Six Days* (Canon Press, 1999), 211-226.

It seems the primary rationale to de-historicize Genesis is what Steve Boyd explains in the film. He observes, "the only way you'd want *yom* [day] to mean a longer period of time is if you impose an alien concept, a hermeneutical concept, to the text and say, 'Well, I think that these are ages therefore *yom* has to mean ages.' What we have to do is start with the text. If we start with the text *yom* means 'day.'"

This desire to impose 'an alien concept' on Genesis is extremely strong today, especially in academic circles. We should therefore not underestimate its pervasive influence on the church, nor mistake its long-term consequences. The Bible's ability to accurately represent history is at the center of Christian doctrine, most particularly the doctrine of creation; it is this doctrine which sits at the foundation of all our theology.

God created the universe out of nothing by the power of His word; this reveals His transcendent power. Nevertheless, He created everything in order for men and women to be able to walk with Him and know Him; this reveals His immanent presence.

Read Psalm 33:1-9

The psalmist calls us to worship God and to give Him thanks.

- What are his reasons we should do this? *it is fitting*

- What are some of the things we learn about God's word in this passage? *it is right, true*
- What are the similarities between Psalm 33 and the creation account for Day 1 and 3?

- What should be the response of the people of the earth who behold God's creation? *fear Him, revere Him*

One of the most important results of considering God's creation is to praise Him and worship Him. Take some time today to look at the world around you and give Him praise for what He has done.

Pray that God would open your eyes to see the wonderful things He has done in His creation.

God created everything in six normal days to provide a structure of time for man to live by. In other words, time was made for man, not man for time.

Read Exodus 31:12-18

It is interesting to note that the last thing we hear God say to Moses before He hands him the stone tablets is a short discourse on the Sabbath.

- Why do you think God returns to the Sabbath as the final thing He wants Moses to tell the people? *It was the end of creation It is Holy — so we may know God*

- How serious is it that the people observe the Sabbath? *Will be cut off — put to death if you dont — it was a Covenant*

- Why does God make such a point of drawing a comparison between the first week of creation/rest and all the weeks afterward?

- Is it still important to observe rest on the Christian Sabbath (Sunday)? Why or why not?

- In the gospels, we see Jesus heal a man on the Sabbath and provide his disciples with food. How does this relate to the idea of the Sabbath as a day of restoration for God's people?

The Sabbath is ultimately a gift from God for our use. We were designed to work and rest in the pattern He provided for us.

Pray that God would give you the ability to follow His pattern of work and rest each week.

God's original creation was 'very good' and operated on a different set of relationships than we currently experience. In His goodness, God provided Adam and Eve everything they would need to know and worship Him.

Read Isaiah 11:1-9

This is Isaiah's vision of the future kingdom of God as led by Christ, the "shoot from the stump of Jesse." It is a picture of a world completely different from the one we now know which is currently defined by unrighteousness and natural evil.

- Describe some of the aspects of this new world that is coming. — *Christ will fairly judge — all animals will coexist in harmony*

- Why is the description of animal relationships so extraordinary to us? What is Isaiah assuming that we know about the world we live in?

- How is the knowledge of God related to a world that is at peace with each other?

- Although we don't currently experience a world like this, why is it possible for us to imagine one like it?

- What does verse 9 say is the goal of this new world? *— to be full of the knowledge of the Lord.*

Ultimately, this is a view of the new heavens and the new earth talked about in Revelation 21. It is a return to a world without sin and death. It is something wonderful to look forward to.

Pray that God would give us the grace to act in peace and kindness to all those who are around us, in anticipation of the peace of heaven.

Ron - traveling to
Africa - 3 wks
   health

Mark & Jan - P.R.

John - pain in foot

Phyllis - went to ER - heart
palpitations
   Back Dr. Feb 29
Parkinsons - had for 5 mo.

   Wisdom for Drs.

3

Man, Life, & Science

The Doctrine of the Image of God

"*Science is a means of better understanding God's creation so that we can serve him by meeting the needs of that creation.*"

— KURT WISE

Read Genesis 1:11-13, 20-31

And God said, "Let the earth sprout vegetation, plants yielding seed, and fruit trees bearing fruit in which is their seed, each according to its kind, on the earth." And it was so...

And God said, "Let the waters swarm with swarms of living creatures, and let birds fly above the earth across the expanse of the heavens." So God created the great sea creatures and every living creature that moves, with which the waters swarm, according to their kinds, and every winged bird according to its kind...

And God said, "Let the earth bring forth living creatures according to their kinds—livestock and creeping things and beasts of the earth according to their kinds." And it was so...

Then God said, "Let us make man in our image, after our likeness. And let them have dominion over the fish of the sea and over the birds of the heavens and over the livestock and over all the earth and over every creeping thing that creeps on the earth."

So God created man in his own image, in the image of God he created him; male and female he created them.

And God blessed them. And God said to them, "Be fruitful and multiply and fill the earth and subdue it, and have dominion over the fish of the sea and over the birds of the heavens and over every living thing that moves on the earth."

And God said, "Behold, I have given you every plant yielding seed that is on the face of all the earth, and every tree with seed in its fruit. You shall have them for food. And to every beast of the earth and to every bird of the heavens and to everything that creeps on the earth, everything that has the breath of life, I have given every green plant for food." And it was so. And God saw everything that he had made, and behold, it was very good. And there was evening and there was morning, the sixth day.

Ask Questions

- What does God mean when He says He made plants and animals "according to their kind?"

- What does it mean that God made man in His image?

Ask Questions

- How has God filled the world with life? Why has He done this?

- Kurt talks about "mutualism" where one thing is dependent on another in various interconnected relationships. How does that pattern reflect the way we are to live in the church? In our society?

- What does Kurt say science is?

- How is the pursuit of science a unique expression of being made in God's image? Why is it important for Christians to pursue science?

The Doctrine of the Image of God

Genesis provides the reason we are unique in comparison to all the other living creatures: our first father and mother were created in the image of God. As their children, we bear that same image.

Although God filled the world with plants, birds, fish, and animals, each created according to its kind, He made Man like Himself and appointed him the head of creation.

There have been different ideas throughout the history of the church as to what exactly the image of God consists of.

What is the *image of God?*

The image of God is the unique spiritual quality that people share with God, such as a moral nature, rationality, intelligence, and the ability to express the fruits of the Spirit, particularly love.

Why did God create Adam and Eve in His image?

He did so in order to have a loving, personal, and worshipful relationship with them that was unique from the angelic orders to the animals. God desires the same relationship with each of us.

Here are some things the Bible teaches about the image of God:

1 Adam and Eve were created in God's image, fully-formed, so they could fulfill their work of understanding, manipulating, and overseeing the creation under God's personal involvement.

Read Genesis 2:4-8

These are the generations of the heavens and the earth when they were created, in the day that the LORD God made the earth and the heavens.

When no bush of the field was yet in the land and no small plant of the field had yet sprung up—for the LORD God had not caused it to rain on the land, and there was no man to work the ground, and a mist was going up from the land and was watering the whole face of the ground— then the LORD God formed the man of dust from the ground and breathed into his nostrils the breath of life, and the man became a living creature. And the LORD God planted a garden in Eden, in the east, and there he put the man whom he had formed.

The LORD God took the man and put him in the garden of Eden to work it and keep it. And the LORD God commanded the man, saying, "You may surely eat of every tree of the garden, but of the tree of the knowledge of good and evil you shall not eat, for in the day that you eat of it you shall surely die."

Then the LORD God said, "It is not good that the man should be alone; I will make him a helper fit for him." Now out of the ground the LORD God had formed every beast of the field and every bird of the heavens and brought them to the man to see what he would call them. And whatever the man called every living creature, that was its name. The man gave names to all livestock and to the birds of the heavens and to every beast of the field. But for Adam there was not found a helper fit for him.

So the LORD God caused a deep sleep to fall upon the man, and while he slept took one of his ribs and closed up its place with flesh. And the rib that the LORD God had taken from the man he made into a woman and brought her to the man. Then the man said,

"This at last is bone of my bones and flesh of my flesh; she shall be called Woman, because she was taken out of Man."

Therefore a man shall leave his father and his mother and hold fast to his wife, and they shall become one flesh. And the man and his wife were both naked and were not ashamed.

What do we see about the image of God in Adam at the beginning?

- Adam has unique intellectual and **relational capabilities,** including the ability to communicate, to reason, and to love.

- Adam has unique **moral capabilities,** including the ability to obey or disobey God's instructions.

- Adam has unique **dominion capabilities,** including the ability to discern the purpose and nature of animals.

What are some of the mutual relationships God established at the beginning?

- **The relationship of parental authority between Adam and God.** As Luke tells us, Adam is *"the son of God"* (Luke 3:38) God therefore meets Adam's every need and want. Yet, because Adam was made in God's image, he could have a submissive relationship with Him that would involve working together with Eve to fill the earth. As God commands them: *"Be fruitful and multiply and fill the earth and subdue it."*

- **The relationship of dominion between Adam and the animals.** In the Hebrew culture, a name reflected the essence of something or someone; he who was naming demonstrated control over that which was named. In this case, Adam has the God-given ability to perceive the unique natures of the different kinds of animals and identify the purposes for which they were designed. It is therefore not surprising that people have relied on animals for work and mutual relationships throughout all of history.

- **The relationship of communion between Adam and Eve.** They were designed to work together and bring comfort and happiness to each other as they relate to one another and to God. Marriage between one man and one woman under God's direction is therefore the foundation of all civilization.

- **The relationship of future children who would grow up to be men and women themselves.** Jesus identified Genesis 2 as the first marriage in Matthew 19. The fact that the two would become one flesh meant they were expected to have children according to their kind. This looked forward to a world of relationships between people all designed to work under God in His creation.

If science is the study and knowledge of the natural world in order to understand and control it, why can Adam be viewed as the first scientist?

God created a world that Adam could look into, understand, and thereby grow in his knowledge of. God gave Adam the ability to identify different aspects of the world around him in an orderly way. Adam is therefore identifying creatures according to their unique attributes. He is the forefather of the great 18th-century Christian scientist Carl Linnaeus who established the modern system of naming animals known as taxonomy.

In naming the creatures by examining them, Adam was defining each animal by its characteristics. An accurate name gave him the ability to predict what it would do as well as to control it. For instance, if someone tells us they see a 'dog' then there numerous things we can assume and predict about that creature; knowing what a dog is helps us to use and control it. The same goes with a bear, duck, or cat, all examples of created kinds.

2 There is a hierarchy to the created universe. Man is a little lower than the angelic orders and his role as God's image-bearer is to steward those creatures that have been put under him.

Read Psalm 8:3-9

When I look at your heavens, the work of your fingers, the moon and the stars, which you have set in place, what is man that you are mindful of him, and the son of man that you care for him?

Yet you have made him a little lower than the heavenly beings and crowned him with glory and honor. You have given him dominion over the works of your hands; you have put all things under his feet, all sheep and oxen, and also the beasts of the field, the birds of the heavens, and the fish of the sea, whatever passes along the paths of the seas.

O LORD, our Lord, how majestic is your name in all the earth!

Is it possible to reconcile evolutionary theory with what Psalm 8 says about the place of man in relationship to angels and other creatures?

The Psalmist surveys all aspects of creation, from the heavens to the animals, and recognizes the uniqueness of man. He stands out from the rest of creation because He was made in God's image. Evolutionary theory, however, would see man as being just one expression of living beings, essentially connected to all other living beings through common descent.

Is it possible to reconcile evolutionary theory with what Genesis 1 tells us about created kinds being instantly created and fully-formed?

One of the principal tenets of modern evolutionary theory is the common ancestry of all living creatures. This is represented by the evolutionary "tree of life" with its branches connected down through time to a single starting point. The tree of life illustrates the progressive, slowly-changing, and interconnected relationships between all living creatures. The Bible, on the other hand, presents all living creatures as having been created within a few days of each other, fully-formed, each according to its kind.

Is it possible to reconcile the evolution of man with what Genesis 2 tells us about the historical creation of Adam & Eve?

Theories about the evolution of man describe a history of development taking many millions of years. It is a history filled with the slow progression and countless deaths of ape-like creatures trying to evolve into the first human. This is a completely different history than the one recorded in the Bible in which Adam is formed from the dust as a fully-grown man, then Eve is formed from Adam's rib as a fully-grown woman. There is no way to reconcile these two histories.

What is the proper way for us to take care of the creation under God?

Man has sometimes been referred to as a "steward" of God's creation. In other words, he is meant to take care of it on behalf of God. We are to use the creation, and conserve it for other generations. This includes supervision of living things and balancing their use in Biblically-informed and generationally-sustainable ways. There are many principles in the Mosaic law concerning agriculture and the proper treatment of animals. This is the best place to begin.

What happens when we replace the word "creation" with the word "environment"?

The word creation naturally points back to the Creator, and links everything to the history recorded in Genesis. The word "environment" potentially detaches the natural world from its Creator. Furthermore, the environment can be elevated to a place above man, resulting in imbalanced decisions and approaches to the creation and man's stewardship of it.

There are two extremes that we see today in regard to the way we treat God's creation:

- What is the problem with elevating the natural world above man, as some environmentalists do? What are the consequences when the creation becomes an object of worship?

- What is the problem with making the natural world the slave of man, as those who pollute or abuse natural resources do? Has the creation become something to be consumed instead of properly stewarded?

These are complex issues in the modern world, but the only solution is to look at them with Biblical wisdom in light of God giving us dominion over the creation. The realm of science gives us knowledge of the creation in order to steward it to the best of our abilities.

3 Man, who is the image of God, must be protected from other evil men and beasts who would seek to destroy that image. Instead, God wants to increase the number of people on the earth in order to fill the world with His image.

Read Genesis 9:5-7

"And for your lifeblood I will require a reckoning: from every beast I will require it and from man. From his fellow man I will require a reckoning for the life of man. 'Whoever sheds the blood of man, by man shall his blood be shed, for God made man in his own image.' And you, be fruitful and multiply, increase greatly on the earth and multiply in it."

Verse 6 is the institution of the death penalty for men and animals who kill a man. Why is this localized judgment necessary?

Murder is Satan's primary tool to attempt to stop God's purposes from being accomplished. Jesus Himself explained that Satan was a *"murderer from the beginning."* (John 8:44) In the early history of man, we see murder as both the first and last sin mentioned in Cain's line. As a result of this threat, the image of God must be protected in societies through laws and punishment.

In the film *Is Genesis History?*, Dr. Marcus Ross talked about the extreme violence seen in the fossil record from the time before the Flood. Although we don't know the exact situation in which humans were living at the time, nor how many were actually living on the earth, it is clear from God's comments in Genesis 6 that both human and animal kingdoms were incredibly violent: *"Now the earth was corrupt in God's sight, and the earth was filled with violence."* This is why animals that kill people must themselves be killed in order to protect the image of God. God's distinction continues to highlight the significant difference between man and the other creatures He made.

There are repetitions between what God said to Adam in the garden and what God said to Noah after he left the ark. Why does God repeat Himself?

God's purpose for making man in His image has always been to fill the earth with His image-bearers. That was the original intent with Adam and his children, and it continues to be the intent with Noah and his children. It is why children are always a good thing: they are new examples of God filling the world with His image.

What does being made in God's image mean for our dignity and for the way we treat other people? How does this contrast with the view of man if he is a product of evolution?

We recognize the innate dignity of all people because we are unique creations designed to reflect God's glory. As Paul says, *"[man] is the image and glory of God."* (1 Corinthians 11:7) This is the opposite of the evolutionary view of man which sees him as being made in the image of lower animals. It is an essential distinction between the two views of history, and each has logical consequences for our culture.

What are the implications that flow out of the acceptance of a Biblical view of man's nature versus the evolutionary view of man's nature in a culture, especially in terms of life? Of sexuality? Of morality? Of psychology?

Explore what this means in terms of questions about abortion and euthanasia; of the place of sex, homosexuality, and gender; of the way people are treated in business; of taking care of the poor; of the approach of dealing with psychological and emotional problems; and many others.

Closing Thoughts

When we start with the doctrine that man is made in the image of God, it not only determines who we are as people, but it influences the choices we make in society concerning basic issues of life and culture. It is important to see how the doctrine of the image of God is foundational to every aspect of our lives.

Creation Accounts in Genesis 1 & 2

Some commentators have argued Genesis 1 and 2 present different—even contradictory—creation accounts. For instance, they have asked:

- Why is there a new introduction to creation given in Genesis 2:4?

- How could there not be any plants of the field in Genesis 2:5 if God created all the plants on Day 3?

- How could all the things listed in Genesis 2 happen in one normal day?

These are reasonable questions, and throughout the history of the church, reasonable answers have been given. The following is a summary of some of those answers.

What is the relationship between Genesis 1:1-2:3 and Genesis 2:4-4:26?

In Genesis 1-2:3, Moses gives an overview of the first week of creation. In Genesis 2:4 and following, he shifts his perspective to the events of the sixth day. The words that mark this new section are *"These are the generations of the heavens and the earth when they were created, in the day that the* LORD *made the earth and the heavens."*

The word "generations" marks the first of 10 sections in Genesis which begin with the Hebrew word *toledot* that can also be translated "history" or "descendants." For the next three chapters, Moses records the history of the heavens and the earth in terms of its relationship to Adam and Eve and their children. These chapters show how man's sin and God's curse transformed the heavens and the earth from a beneficent paradise into a fallen world filled with evil.

This section of history is one of the most important in the Bible. It describes God's commands to Adam, the initial relationship between man and animals, the first marriage, and the garden of Eden. It records the sin that led to the corruption and death of the entire human race, as well as the punishment of the serpent alongside the promise of a coming savior. It tells of the first murder, then traces the growth of sin from Cain through his children to the seventh generation, ending in polygamy and further murder.

As is common with Hebrew histories, a general overview comes first and recounts the creation of the entire universe in Genesis 1.[6] This is followed by Moses going back to the creation of Adam and Eve on the sixth day in Genesis 2, then explaining their history forward. (Note the similar pattern in Exodus 1 and 2 with the general introduction of the Israelites and their problem, then the introduction of Moses and his history.)

In spite of this known pattern, some modern commentators continue to question whether chapters 1 and 2 are different creation stories. They point out that different Hebrew words for God's name are used in Genesis 1 and 2; they argue that contradictory natural phenomena are described in the two chapters; and they assert that some of the phenomena described and events listed are impossible.

Why are different uses of God's name given in Chapter 1 vs. Chapter 2:4ff?

In Genesis 1-2:3, the word translated "God" is the Hebrew word *Elohim*. In Genesis 2:4ff, the words translated "LORD God" are the Hebrew words *Yahweh Elohim*.

These are basically two different ways that God describes how He relates to man and the creation. For instance, the word God *(Elohim)* by itself refers to God in His transcendent, all-powerful ruler capacity. The words LORD God *(Yahweh Elohim)* refers to God in His moral and personal capacity.[7]

When seen from this perspective, it makes sense that Genesis 1, which is the story of the creation of the universe and everything in it, would use the name of God that emphasizes His transcendent power. In Genesis 2:4ff, however, God is personally forming man and relating to him, therefore it makes more sense that His immanence is revealed.

---

6   Umberto Cassuto, *A Commentary on the Book of Genesis* (The Magnes Press, 1972), 91.

7   Ibid., 87.

Interestingly, the dialogue between the serpent and the woman uses the name *Elohim*, pointing to the fact that God is not being referred to in a personal capacity but as an all-powerful Creator.[8]

Why does Moses point out that "no bush of the field was yet in the land and no small plant of the field had yet sprung up" at the start of this history? Weren't all the plants created on Day 3?

The words translated "bush of the field" and "small plant of the field" are *siah* and *esebh*. *Esebh* refer to plants like barley, wheat, and other grains that required cultivation by man to grow as crops, which is why Moses points out *"there was no man to work the ground."* When man was created, the ground had not yet been plowed with these and cultivated, although they existed. Moses is showing that the purpose of man is to work the land in relationship with God who will provide water for growth.[9]

The word *siah*, on the other hand, refers to wild-growing plants such as thorns and thistles that grow up naturally and threaten the *esebh*, but which either did not exist before the Fall or were in an unfallen genetic state.

This all becomes apparent after the transgression of Adam when God tells him: "cursed is the ground because of you; in pain you shall eat of it all the days of your life; thorns and thistles (*sihim*, which is related to *siah*) it shall bring forth for you; and you shall eat the plants *(esebh)* of the field. By the sweat of your face you shall eat bread…"[10]

As is often the case in the Bible, words are used as markers to indicate changes in meaning from one usage to the next. The whole section is intended to show how man *should* have lived versus how he *ended up* living. It is the explanation of how the heavens and the earth came to be in a fallen state, now filled with *thorns and thistles.*

---

8   Ibid., 88.

9   Ibid., 101.

10   Ibid., 102.

This passage has nothing to do with the creation of all the plant life of the world, but with specific manifestations of specific plant life, including the garden of Eden, the two trees, and the *siah* and *esebh*.

Why does Moses mention water going up from the ground?

Moses is explaining the way God designed the land to be watered, apparently with phenomena that no longer exist in exactly the same form.

The word *edh* that is translated "mist" or "spring" or "water" is a difficult word to translate. In light of the fact that this water *"waters the whole face of the ground"* (or the whole earth), it must be referring to a massive source of subterranean water.[11] We can imagine such a thing, but don't have any current natural phenomena of that scale to compare it to.

In fact, there are other natural phenomena described in Genesis that are not represented in our world today, such as a garden with a great river flowing out of the ground separating into four major rivers, trees that give knowledge or life, or humans living for hundreds of years. Although some people would like to write these off as mythological stories, they are simply reminders that the world before the Fall and Flood were different places with different natural configurations.

The Bible often relates historical events that are not situations we can relate to, but which are clearly possible under different circumstances.

Was Eden located somewhere near the modern Tigris and Euphrates Rivers?

Following the logic that the Bible presents natural phenomena that no longer exist today, the locations described in this passage were wiped off the earth during the Flood. The enormous layers of sedimentary rock that cover the globe up to three miles thick are testimony to the complete destruction of the pre-Flood world. In fact, almost all of the ancient Mesopotamian cultures are built on top of Flood and post-Flood strata.

---

11   Ibid., 103.

As a result, there is no use trying to locate Eden somewhere in the Middle East or Africa or any other modern location. The area where Eden existed was destroyed in the Flood.

Although some people point to the modern Tigris and Euphrates rivers as two of the rivers mentioned in Genesis 2:10-14, these do not fit the text which describes *one* river separating into four rivers.

The same goes for the lands of Assyria and Cush mentioned in relation to the rivers: it is possible that they shared the same names as their pre-Flood counterparts because they were named by people who knew of the world before the Flood.

When Noah and his sons emerged from the Ark, they and their children spread from the Caucasus region down into the Mesopotamian basin, settling in new lands and discovering new rivers. It is possible they did what people do when they find something new: they name it after something from their past. It is the reason why the United States and Canada have so many locations named after European countries, regions, and towns such as New England, Paris, and London, not to mention ancient places like Athens, Sparta, and Carthage.

This is, however, a mysterious passage that does not seem to fit with anything we know in the current world, although it is described in a way that suggests that it is a real place that the hearers could relate to in some way.

How could all the things described on Day Six happen, including Adam naming all the beasts and birds in one day?

Once one realizes that the makeup of the world was different than our current makeup, it is not difficult to imagine a schedule for the first day. When one combines the events of the sixth day from Genesis 1 with the events recorded in Genesis 2, the following scenario is possible. (Please note that the following exercise is speculative, but shows that time is not a problem for what is described.)[12]

Let's say God started at 6am and created all the beasts of the earth and livestock according to their kinds. Although we don't know how many dif-

---

12 The idea for this exercise came from *Creation in Six Days* by James B. Jordan.

ferent variations on each kind were originally created, the total number of *kinds* would have been similar to those on the ark: perhaps over 1000 different kinds of birds, reptiles, and mammals? (As a point of comparison, there are only approximately 5400 *total* species of mammals that exist today, with perhaps 900 of those species made up of just *one* created kind: bats. In other words, even if the original creation had more created kinds, it is still a relatively small number.)

If it took God one hour to create all the land creatures, that would mean He would have ended with Adam at 7am. Adam could have then watched God take an hour to plant the Garden of Eden with all its fruit trees "springing up" out of the ground rapidly.

It would now be 8am and Adam could have the world's first breakfast as God brought him examples from the animal and bird kingdoms to name. If there were 1000 different kinds, and he named about four each minute, he would be done by noon. He could then have had lunch and talked to God about the animals, then taken an afternoon nap.

God could then have created Eve from Adam's rib and presented her to him at, say, 3pm. They could spend their first afternoon together with God, had dinner, then seen the stars together for the world's first honeymoon.

The point of this *extremely* speculative exercise is simply to show that merging Genesis 1 and 2 does not present any real contradictions. In fact, they fit together exceptionally well.

Adam and Eve were created in God's image, fully-formed, so they could fulfill their work of understanding, manipulating, and overseeing the creation under God's personal involvement.

Read Psalm 90:12-17

This is the end of the psalm of Moses we discussed in Lesson 2. Moses recognizes man is limited in his ability to work due to his sin, weakness, and death. We will look at the fall of man and the curse on creation more closely in the next lesson. For now, Moses talks about the solution to our difficulties with work.

- Why is it important that we learn to "number our days"? What does he mean by this?

- Why is God's love an important part of us being able to complete our work?

- Why is God's involvement in our work important and necessary for our work?

- Why must we ask God to "establish the work of our hands?"

In the original creation order, we were intended to work on the earth with God's continual involvement. Now that we are sinners, we often think we can accomplish our goals without God's involvement. Instead, Moses teaches us that we should understand the place God has put us in and rely on Him to ensure our work is effective and fruitful.

Pray that God would give you wisdom in terms of what you do with your time and that He would establish the work of your hands.

There is a hierarchy to the created universe. Man is a little lower than the angelic orders and his role as God's image-bearer is to steward those creatures and things that have been put underneath him.

Read Psalm 8

This psalm is a song of humbled praise before God for what He has done in the creation. David looks at the world around him, then looks at man's position in it: it is incredible to him that God cares for man at all. Yet he knows God does care, not only because of the way he was made, but because of the position in which God has placed him.

- How does David begin the psalm? Why is it important to begin this way?

- What does looking at the stars make David consider about himself?

- How is David incorporating Genesis 1 into his psalm?

- Why is "dominion" an important aspect of what we do as humans?

- How does being made in God's image fit in with this psalm?

- As you consider your own unique role in the world, what are some reasons you can find to praise God?

The Biblical concept of dominion means to rule over something with service and love, looking out for the best interest of those in our care. We sometimes don't consider our work in the world as one of "dominion," but whether we are raising a family, going to school, or working a job, we have a responsibility to consider how we can work with God to build up His kingdom in the creation.

Pray that God would show you how you can help Him build up His kingdom to reveal His majesty in the world.

Man, who is the image of God, must be protected from other evil men and beasts who would seek to destroy that image. Instead, God wants to increase the number of people on the earth in order to fill the world with countless examples His image.

Read Genesis 9:1-17

There are many parallels between what God tells Noah after he leaves the Ark and what God told Adam after He created him. But there are also many differences. Unlike Adam, Noah was living in a fallen world that had just been catastrophically judged by God.

In one sense, God was starting over with Noah. But because of sin, the situation had significantly changed.

- What is the mission God gives to Noah that is similar to what He told Adam? If Noah and his family are the only images of God left in the world, what does God want to see all over the world?

- What does God tell Noah about food that is different from what He told Adam?

- Why is it important that God promises never to flood the earth again?

- If local floods still occur around the world today, what does that tell us about the flood in Genesis?

- Why does God make His covenant (a solemn agreement) not only with Noah, but with all the living creatures?

- What is the true importance of the rainbow?

When we see the rainbow, we are to remember God's promise of the covenant to Noah and all the creatures of the earth. It is designed to remind us of God's grace and mercy in the midst of great judgment.

Pray the Lord would grant you eyes to see the impact of His grace on your life and in the world around you.

4

Adam, Eve, & the First Sin

The Doctrine of the Fall

"Central to the plan of salvation would be the two Adams, the first Adam and the last Adam."

— DOUGLAS KELLY

Read Genesis 3:17-19

And to Adam he said, "Because you have listened to the voice of your wife and have eaten of the tree of which I commanded you, 'You shall not eat of it,' cursed is the ground because of you; in pain you shall eat of it all the days of your life; thorns and thistles it shall bring forth for you; and you shall eat the plants of the field. By the sweat of your face you shall eat bread, till you return to the ground, for out of it you were taken; for you are dust, and to dust you shall return."

Ask Question

- What does God say are the results of Adam's sin?

Read John 11:25-26

Jesus said to [Martha], "I am the resurrection and the life. Whoever believes in me, though he die, yet shall he live, and everyone who lives and believes in me shall never die."

Ask Question

- What does Jesus say is the result of believing in him?

Read 1 Corinthians 15:21-22

For as by a man came death, by a man has come also the resurrection of the dead. For as in Adam all die, so also in Christ shall all be made alive.

Ask Question

- What is Paul comparing?

Watch Video 4 — "Adam, Eve, & the First Sin"

Douglas Kelly, PhD, Theologian

Ask Questions

- What does it mean that Adam and Jesus are the two primary representatives of the human race?

- Why does it matter whether death and corruption came into the world as a result of Adam's sin rather than existing long before him?

- How important is it that there be a literal Adam who was the first human and whose actions affected the entire human race?

The Doctrine of the Fall

When we studied the doctrine of creation, we saw that God created a world that was "very good." God's command only to eat plants pointed to a world that operated on a different set of natural laws and relationships than we know today. It was a world of harmony, beauty, and plenty without corruption and death as we now know them.

God put Adam in the garden and gave him complete freedom with one prohibition: *"You may surely eat of every tree of the garden, but of the tree of the knowledge of good and evil you shall not eat, for in the day that you eat of it you shall surely die."* (Genesis 2:16-17)

Yet Adam disobeyed God by eating from the tree of the knowledge of good and evil. The doctrine associated with the results of this disobedience is known as "the Fall."

What is *the Fall?*

The Fall refers to Adam and Eve's physical and spiritual separation from God as well as God's curse on His entire creation.

The Fall is the most consequential event in the history of the world before the coming of Jesus Christ. Its reverberating impact is still with us today.

Here are some of the key results:

1 Adam's sin brought death and corruption into the world; as a result, sin, death, and corruption passed to all his children.

The generational results of Adam's sin are the first things we see after the Fall.

Read Genesis 4:3-8

In the course of time Cain brought to the LORD an offering of the fruit of the ground, and Abel also brought of the firstborn of his flock and of their fat portions. And the LORD had regard for Abel and his offering, but for Cain and his offering he had no regard. So Cain was very angry, and his face fell. The LORD said to Cain, "Why are you angry, and why has your face fallen? If you do well, will you not be accepted? And if you do not do well, sin is crouching at the door. Its desire is contrary to you, but you must rule over it." Cain spoke to Abel his brother. And when they were in the field, Cain rose up against his brother Abel and killed him.

Why do Cain and Abel feel the need to offer sacrifices to God? What does that tell us about the changed world they are living in?

Offerings of crops and animals as a sacrifice to God are normally associated with the request that God forgive one's sin. This is a different world than the one in which Adam and Eve were created; it is a world in which the killing of animals is a normal way of life. Cain and Abel were born into a fallen world in which sin had power over their choices. They both knew they needed to approach God for forgiveness and acceptance through sacrifice. As the author of Hebrews points out, *"By faith Abel offered to God a more acceptable sacrifice than Cain, through which he was commended as righteous, God commending him by accepting his gifts."* (Hebrews 11:4) There is nothing meritorious in itself in the act of sacrifice; rather, it is what the act points to and reveals about a person's heart that matters to God.

How does God explain the nature and power of sin to Cain?

It is personified as a wild beast, crouching at his door, seeking to destroy him.

Why does Cain choose to kill Abel if he was angry with God?

Cain could not touch God himself, so he destroyed the image of God that was nearest to him. Because Abel was living righteously, he was a bright reflection of God's nature; as a result, Cain's anger burned against him. He killed him because he could not kill God. The Apostle John explains that: *"We should not be like Cain, who was of the evil one and murdered his brother. And why did he murder him? Because his own deeds were evil and his brother's righteous."* (1 John 3:12)

In the book of Romans, Paul provides additional commentary on the results of Adam's sin.

Read Romans 5:12-14

Therefore, just as sin came into the world through one man, and death through sin, and so death spread to all men because all sinned— for sin indeed was in the world before the law was given, but sin is not counted where there is no law. Yet death reigned from Adam to Moses, even over those whose sinning was not like the transgression of Adam, who was a type of the one who was to come.

According to this passage, when did sin and death enter the world, and what happened when it did?

Death entered the world when Adam sinned in the garden. It then spread to all of Adam's children.

Is it possible for there to have been sin and death in the world prior to Adam's sin?

It is not possible for there to have been sin and death in the world prior to Adam's sin. God's statements in Genesis 1 that the original creation was "good" and "very good," the history of Cain and Abel, and the statement of Paul in Romans 5 about sin and death all reveal that the Fall was the turning point of history when sin and death entered the world.

2 God cursed the world as a result of Adam's sin and introduced corruption and death into the universe.

Read Romans 8:20-23

For the creation was subjected to futility, not willingly, but because of him who subjected it, in hope that the creation itself will be set free from its bondage to corruption and obtain the freedom of the glory of the children of God. For we know that the whole creation has been groaning together in the pains of childbirth until now. And not only the creation, but we ourselves, who have the firstfruits of the Spirit, groan inwardly as we wait eagerly for adoption as sons, the redemption of our bodies.

At what point in history was the creation "subjected to futility" and put in "bondage to corruption?"

When God punished Adam and cursed the ground. Paul is talking about an event that happened in the past, which implies the creation was not subjected to futility or in bondage to corruption before that point. This, of course, is what we see in the glimpses God gives us of life in the garden.

What happened to the physical world at the time of the Fall?

In the film *Is Genesis History?*, Kurt Wise talks about God changing the rules of the universe when He cursed the creation; in another place, Marcus Ross talks about potential genetic modifications of the created order, such as thorns and thistles, as a result of the curse. It is difficult to understand exactly what happened to the world since God does not specifically tell us. We can, however, study the modern world and try to reason back to what it would have been like before the Fall. It is like looking through a dim mirror.

Does the Bible provide a good explanation for 'natural evil'?

Natural evil is the condition of suffering, disease, and death that we find affecting all living creatures in the natural world. It is something we all intrinsically know is bad, whether we see animals or people suffer or die. The Bible provides the best explanation for natural evil and our 'unnatural' response to it. After all, if suffering and death are the way it has always been, we should not react so dramatically to them. Rather, our reactions are a result of us knowing that the creation was not originally created this way, but has been put in bondage to corruption.

Why is it difficult for us to accept something we cannot explain?

There is a tendency for people who have grown up in a culture that seeks only physical explanations for events to think that if one can't explain something 'scientifically,' it must not have happened. If this principle is applied consistently throughout the Bible, however, many events recorded in it must be rejected. Instead, the better approach is to recognize the enormous limitations of our knowledge. It is wise to accept the historical accuracy of the

Biblical account, even if we can't understand exactly how it happened. As Hamlet points out to his friend, "There are more things in heaven and earth than are in your philosophy, Horatio."

How is the Biblical history different from the conventional history of the world? Are they compatible?

The Biblical history presents Adam's sin as the transformative event in the natural world, ushering in universal death and corruption. This means sinless, undying humans historically preceded sinful, dying humans. The conventional history of the world, however, has corruption and death precede the appearance of humans. This means Adam's sin would have had no transformative effect on the world: death and corruption would have been present for billions of years. These are two extremely different histories of the world.

3 **Jesus Christ came as "the second Adam" to bring life to those who are dead, as well as to transform the world into a new heavens and earth.**

Read Romans 5:15-18

For if many died through one man's trespass, much more have the grace of God and the free gift by the grace of that one man Jesus Christ abounded for many. And the free gift is not like the result of that one man's sin. For the judgment following one trespass brought condemnation, but the free gift following many trespasses brought justification. For if, because of one man's trespass, death reigned through that one man, much more will those who receive the abundance of grace and the free gift of righteousness reign in life through the one man Jesus Christ. Therefore, as one trespass led to condemnation for all men, so one act of righteousness leads to justification and life for all men. For as by the one man's disobedience the many were made sinners, so by the one man's obedience the many will be made righteous.

List out some of the comparisons Paul is making.

*   Adam's sin/Jesus' righteousness
*   disobedience bringing death/obedience bringing life

- receiving death/receiving life
- judgment following sin brought death to many/free gift following obedience bringing justification for many, etc.

What is the relationship between the historical sin of Adam and the historical death and resurrection of Jesus?

Jesus came as a result of Adam's sin. Had Adam not sinned and brought death and corruption on the entire human race, Jesus would not have needed to come to earth, live a life of complete obedience, die as a sinner, then be raised from the dead in righteousness. Jesus came as the 'second Adam' to save his children from eternal death. This is why miracles of healing and relief from suffering marked Jesus' entire ministry: He was demonstrating His ability to return people to what they were created to be.

In light of this passage, what difference does it make whether Adam was a real person? What difference does it make whether Jesus was a real person?

Every aspect of the gospel of salvation hinges on the historical reality of both Adam and Jesus. They are the two most important men in history.

Peter tells us: *"But according to his promise we are waiting for new heavens and a new earth in which righteousness dwells."* (2 Peter 3:13) Why does Peter draw a connection between the new heavens and earth and righteousness?

Righteousness marked the original heavens and earth, so it will mark the new heavens and earth to be revealed upon Christ's return. The world in which we live is clearly not filled with righteousness. Peter is encouraging us to look forward to a return to something even greater than before.

Closing Thoughts:

The doctrine of the Fall is a very important doctrine for understanding the world around us. Suffering, disease, and death are all a result of Adam's sin, and no one has to tell us that they are a corruption of the original good creation: we intrinsically know it. This is also why we know that we need a Savior to come and provide us relief from suffering and death, and to give us new life. As Paul says, we gain "much more" than was lost: *For if many died through one man's trespass, much more have the grace of God and the free gift by the grace of that one man Jesus Christ abounded for many.*

Theistic Evolution

The evolutionary history of the world teaches that all living creatures are the result of common descent from a single-celled ancestor billions of years ago. This view says that the slow process of random mutations alongside natural selection produced all the life we see around us, including human life. The majority of those who hold this view would consider themselves *atheistic* evolutionists.

Since the time of Charles Darwin, however, some Christians have tried to merge evolutionary theory with the actions of the God of the Bible. They say that God used the process of evolution to create all living organisms. Those who hold this view are called *theistic* evolutionists.

Recently, theistic evolution has grown in popularity due to its acceptance by some leading evangelical pastors and theologians. They would assert that Genesis 1 does not refer to six normal days of creation, and that the flood recorded in Genesis 6-8 was a local, rather than global, event. In these views, they are no different than other old earth creationists.

Who are the other people Cain is referring to in Genesis 4?

An important distinction to theistic evolution, however, is their assertion that there were humans or human-like creatures on the earth along with Adam, Eve, Cain and Abel. One of the observations they make in regard to Genesis 4 is the presence of other people at the time Cain killed Abel. They say these people are testimony to other humans that had evolved along with Cain and Abel. A closer reading of the text, however, reveals that an evolutionary interpretation is unnecessary when one reads Genesis 4 and 5 together.

In Genesis 4, after Cain kills Abel, he voices to God his fear of others finding and killing him. In other words, he is fearful of blood retribution, something common throughout all cultures of the world even up to the present. Where did these people come from? They were other descendants of Adam and Eve, since it appears Cain murdered Abel *over a century* after they had been born. Note that:

1. Adam does not have Seth until he is 130. (Genesis 5:3) Since Seth is the replacement for Abel, it makes sense that Adam and Eve had him soon after Abel was killed, as Eve explains: *"God has appointed for me another offspring instead of Abel, for Cain killed him."* (Genesis 4:25) This puts both Cain and Abel potentially over 100 years old each when Abel died.

2. Cain and Abel would have married their sisters or nieces in order to have children. This had not yet been forbidden by God, possibly because there were no major genetic mutations so near the Fall. In time, cousins would have married cousins resulting in many hundreds of people in the world (if not more) by the time of the first murder. The reason Cain would have been scared of these people is that some would have been related to Abel (such as his sons, grandsons, and nephews) and would therefore have had a good reason to kill him in retribution for their kinsman's death.

3. Biblical authors follow a pattern of stating only what is necessary for advancing their point rather than giving an exhaustive history. The gospel writers write in the same manner, in some instances omitting people and events included by other gospel authors.

In light of this, there is a more textually consistent explanation for the people living in the world when Cain killed Abel than resorting to theistic evolution to explain their presence.

Comparing Genesis & Evolution

Nevertheless, the pressure to accept the conventional history of the world and its evolutionary processes is compelling to some Christians. Let's ask a few additional questions in regard to it:

Why is the conventional, evolutionary view of history incompatible with the history recorded in Genesis?

1. According to Genesis, God created animals, birds, and plants fully-formed and unique as "created kinds." Although there is great genetic potential for change within kinds, created kinds themselves are distinct. According to theistic evolution, there is a long, progressive connection of all living creatures that can be represented in one tree of life.

2. According to Genesis, Adam was immediately made in the image of God, and Eve was made from Adam; both of them were created fully-formed. Mankind therefore occupies a unique position in the creation and has no direct relationship to any other created kinds. According to theistic evolution, however, man is just a higher-order primate, directly related to other modern primates through an extinct common ancestor.

3. According to Genesis, death entered the world with the sin of Adam. This means there was no death in the world prior to Adam's sin. Yet, according to theistic evolution, death was an essential part of the world prior to Adam's sin. As a part of natural selection, death is one of the mechanisms necessary for the evolution of all species.

Of course, it is not only Genesis that states this, but New Testament authors confirm and expand on the history recorded in Genesis.

What does Paul say about Adam and Eve that can be applied to questions of theistic evolution?

1. *"For Adam was formed first, then Eve; and Adam was not deceived, but the woman was deceived and became a transgressor."* (1 Timothy 2:13-14)

2. *"Therefore, just as sin came into the world through one man, and death through sin, and so death spread to all men because all sinned— for sin indeed was in the world before the law was given, but sin is not counted where there is no law. Yet death reigned from Adam to Moses, even over those whose sinning was not like the transgression of Adam, who was a type of the one who was to come."* (Romans 5:12-14 — note that Paul identifies the reign of death starting with Adam)

3. *"Thus it is written, 'The first man Adam became a living being'; the last Adam became a life-giving spirit."* (1 Corinthians 15:45 — note Paul is quoting Genesis 2:7 as an historical authority)

4. *"The first man was from the earth, a man of dust; the second man is from heaven."* (1 Corinthians 15:47)

What does Jesus say about Adam and Eve that can be applied to questions of theistic evolution?

1. *"Have you not read that he who created them from the beginning made them male and female,..."* (Matthew 19:4 — note that Jesus quotes Genesis 1 as a historical authority)

2. *"But from the beginning of creation, 'God made them male and female.'"* (Mark 10:6 — parallel passage, but different wording)

In spite of these statements, some still argue that Paul and Jesus were speaking within the cultural, scientific, and historical context that they knew. This argument, of course, can be applied in reverse to those who are speaking within their contemporary cultural, scientific, and historical context to re-interpret Jesus and Paul.

Instead, as these examples show, there is a reliance upon the witness in Genesis by both Jesus and Paul as *historically authoritative* and thus providing limits on what actually happened. The principle of scripture interpreting scripture must be applied here: Jesus and Paul establish that the normal reading of Genesis 1 and 2 as the instantaneous creation of Adam and Eve as the first humans is the accurate interpretation. These verses tell us that death entered the world with Adam, and that the creation was only cursed after that.

In sum, there is simply no way to merge theistic evolution with the witness of Scripture as to what actually happened in history. They are incompatible.

Adam's sin brought death and corruption into the world; as a result, sin, death, and corruption passed to all his children.

Read Genesis 4:17-5:24

This is the official history of Adam's two lines through seven generations: one descending from Cain to Lamech and another descending from Seth to Enoch (and eventually to Noah). A comparison of these lines side-by-side provides an interesting perspective on the results of Adam's sin.

- How does the growth of sin culminate in Cain's line?

- With Cain's descendant Lamech, we see him taking pride in both polygamy and murder. What does that tell us about the growing power of sin?

- In the line of Seth, we see men who are *"calling on the name of the LORD."* What does that mean?

- Even though there is greater faithfulness to God in the line of Seth, and even though their long lives seem amazing to us, notice the refrain of *"and he died"* at the end of each of their lives. Why does the author do this, and what does it tell us?

- What do you make of the life of Enoch? The unique mark of his life is that he *"walked with God"* and then *"God took him."* Why do you think he did not experience death?

The author of Hebrews explains what happened to Enoch and why: *By faith Enoch was taken up so that he should not see death, and he was not found, because God had taken him. Now before he was taken he was commended as having pleased God. And without faith it is impossible to please him, for whoever would draw near to God must believe that he exists and that he rewards those who seek him.* (Hebrews 11:5-6)

Pray that God would give you the faith of Enoch to draw near to God and walk with Him.

God cursed the world as a result of Adam's sin and introduced corruption and death into the universe.

Read Revelation 20:10-22:5

If you consider the complete history of the universe from beginning to end, there is an interesting parallel structure between the first chapters of Genesis and the last chapters of Revelation. In Genesis 1, God creates the heavens and the earth, then describes it as being *"very good."* In Genesis 2, we see the creation of the Garden of Eden and the marriage of Adam and Eve. In Genesis 3, Moses recounts Satan's victory, the fall of man, the entry of death into the world, and the curse on creation.

That historical structure is reversed in the final chapters of the book of Revelation. In Revelation 20, we see the final punishment of Satan and his followers, including the destruction of death. In Revelation 21 and 22, we see the restoration of the heavens and the earth as a garden city with a great river flowing out of it; we see the marriage of Christ and his Bride; and we see the light of God replacing the sun and moon as all the faithful children of Adam and Eve worship God eternally.

- What does this intentional pattern tell us about history and what God is doing with it?

- According to this passage, are some of the laws of the universe different in the new heavens and earth? What are some of the differences?

- There are a lot of things we cannot comprehend about this language, but why should we not discount what it says simply because we cannot understand it?

This very important parallel between the first and last chapters of the Bible should remind us that God has intentionally structured time and the events of history. Nothing is accidental.

Pray that God would give us faith to trust the words He has delivered to us in the Bible.

Jesus Christ came as "the second Adam" to bring life to those who are dead, as well as to transform the world into a new heavens and earth.

Read 1 Corinthians 15:42-57

The relationship between the actions of Adam and the actions of Jesus is at the center of the gospel. There are many different aspects of this comparison, so Paul takes time to explain to the Corinthians the important differences between these two men concerning where we are now and where we will eventually be:

- Paul compares the burial of the dead to a seed being sown; it will grow up into something completely new and different. Consider Christ's body before and after His resurrection—what insight does that give us to what Paul is saying?

- If we are originally made of things that will perish, what will we one day be made of?

- When will all these things happen?

- Why is it important that Death be *"swallowed up in victory?"* Why is Death the real enemy of man?

- If the first man was not victorious over death, why is it that we can be victorious? Where does our victory come from?

Again, we are presented with a situation that is beyond our natural abilities to comprehend. Paul takes great pains to try to make comparisons with things we can relate to, but there is a limit to what we can understand in our current natural states. As he points out earlier in the same letter, *"no eye has seen, nor ear heard, nor the heart of man imagined, what God has prepared for those who love him."* (1 Corinthians 2:9)

Pray that God would give us the power of Christ's resurrection to live in our natural bodies as we look forward to one day being set free from this body of sin and death.

5

The Global Flood
The Doctrine of Judgment

*"Aside from the crucifixion accounts in the gospels,
Genesis 7 is the worst chapter of the Bible."*

— MARCUS ROSS

Read 2 Peter 3:1-7

This is now the second letter that I am writing to you, beloved. In both of them I am stir-ring up your sincere mind by way of reminder, that you should remember the predictions of the holy prophets and the commandment of the Lord and Savior through your apostles, knowing this first of all, that scoffers will come in the last days with scoffing, following their own sinful desires. They will say, "Where is the promise of his coming? For ever since the fathers fell asleep, all things are continuing as they were from the beginning of creation." For they deliberately overlook this fact, that the heavens existed long ago, and the earth was formed out of water and through water by the word of God, and that by means of these the world that then existed was deluged with water and perished. But by the same word the heavens and earth that now exist are stored up for fire, being kept until the day of judgment and destruction of the ungodly.

Ask Questions

• What is it that scoffers are really saying with their comments?

• What are the three major events in world history which are being over-looked by scoffers?

Watch Video 5 — "The Global Judgment of God"
Marcus Ross, PhD, Paleontologist

Ask Questions

• How often do we think about the judgment of God today?

• Why is it important to Peter that the Flood be a real, global event?

• Depending on where we live, many of us regularly pass road cuts that reveal enormous layers of rock. In light of the global Flood, what are these a constant reminder of?

• What is our only hope for salvation in light of the coming global Judgment?

The Doctrine of Judgment

The Judgment of God is not a popular subject today. Although it has rarely been popular, prior generations took it much more seriously.

What is God's *judgment?*

God's judgment is His just action in history to punish disobedience and sin.

The results of God's judgment can be seen throughout the Bible. He punishes individuals (King Uzziah stricken with leprosy for sacrificing in the temple), families (Achan and his entire family stoned for Achan's sin), communities (raining fire on Sodom and Gomorrah for their sins), nations (the destruction of Israel and Judah for their continual disobedience), or the entire earth (the global flood of Noah's day).

As Paul says, *"the judgment of God rightly falls on those who practice such things."* (Romans 2:2)

In fact, it is the anticipation of God's coming judgment that begins John the Baptist's ministry: *"Even now the axe is laid to the root of the trees. Every tree therefore that does not bear good fruit is cut down and thrown into the fire."* (Matthew 3:10)

As Peter points out, however, there is a great desire for some "to overlook" the fact that God judged the entire world with water in the past. They do this so they so can also overlook the fact that He will judge the entire world again with fire.

There are three main points to consider:

1 God judged the entire world in the past with the global flood of Noah's day.

Read Genesis 7:11-22

Now the earth was corrupt in God's sight, and the earth was filled with violence. And God saw the earth, and behold, it was corrupt, for all flesh had corrupted their way on the earth. And God said to Noah, "I have determined to make an end of all flesh, for the earth is filled with violence through them. Behold, I will destroy them with the earth.

Make yourself an ark of gopher wood. Make rooms in the ark, and cover it inside and out with pitch. This is how you are to make it: the length of the ark 300 cubits, its breadth 50 cubits, and its height 30 cubits. Make a roof for the ark, and finish it to a cubit above, and set the door of the ark in its side. Make it with lower, second, and third decks. For behold, I will bring a flood of waters upon the earth to destroy all flesh in which is the breath of life under heaven. Everything that is on the earth shall die. But I will establish my covenant with you, and you shall come into the ark, you, your sons, your wife, and your sons' wives with you. And of every living thing of all flesh, you shall bring two of every sort into the ark to keep them alive with you. They shall be male and female. Of the birds according to their kinds, and of the animals according to their kinds, of every creeping thing of the ground, according to its kind, two of every sort shall come in to you to keep them alive. Also take with you every sort of food that is eaten, and store it up. It shall serve as food for you and for them." Noah did this; he did all that God commanded him.

Consider the prior chapters of Genesis 4-6. What does corruption and violence look like in the human world?

It is marked by the violent destruction of God's image by men and animals through murder. The corruption and perversion of God's good creation had reached a level that necessitated it being completely wiped out.

From examining the fossil record of dinosaurs, birds, marine creatures, and other animals, what does that corruption and violence look like in the animal kingdom?

It was a destructive world that seems to have been ruled by powerful and violent reptiles in the air, on the land, and in the sea. Many of the creatures seen in the fossil record have a great fierceness to them, and the record of animal carnivory is extremely strong.

There are a lot of universal words used in Genesis 7: *"the earth was filled with violence," "end of all flesh," "destroy all flesh in which is the breath of life under heaven," "everything...shall die,"* and others. Why is a global judgment necessary to fulfill God's desire to kill every living creature on the earth?

Since animals are designed to fill niches in an ecosystem, if God desires to kill all animals, He will have to destroy all ecosystems. To do that requires a global judgment: water is the best choice. It is a cleansing agent that wipes out all life while only transforming and not destroying the material of the earth. Fire, on the other hand, destroys everything.

Based on measurements of a cubit being 1.5 to 1.75 feet, the Ark was approximately 450 to 525 feet long, 75 to 85 feet wide, and 45 to 50 feet high. It likely had a draft (the part of the ship underneath the water) of 20 to 25 feet. For context, there are some modern ocean-going vessels that are not that large. What does the size of the Ark suggest in terms of a flood?

It suggests a vessel designed to float safely in an ocean-type environment. From a marine engineering perspective, this is a craft designed to sit well in the water and tolerate tumultuous seas. Furthermore, with three decks, it had enormous storage potential. This is exactly the kind of craft necessary for surviving a global flood.

Why does God tell Noah to save two of every "kind" of land and air creature?

As Dr. Todd Wood discusses in the film *Is Genesis History?*, God appears to have put the genetic blueprints for all varieties of animals within each kind. This way, Noah only had to save less than two thousand kinds of animals to save the one set of blueprints for every land and air creature that was to survive the flood. It seems that after the flood, due to changes in the environment and possibly other influencing factors, the animals diversified in new and original ways not necessarily the same as before the Flood. It also appears that some of those creatures, such as dinosaurs, did not survive in this new environment.

How do we see God's salvation and grace in the midst of His judgment?

Genesis 6:8 says: *But Noah found favor in the eyes of the LORD.* The favor that God bestows on Noah and his family is the grace of salvation. Without God's direction and help, Noah can do nothing to save himself. God therefore tells Noah the conditions for salvation, provides him the time and means to construct it, then shuts him and his family inside it. During the Flood, God clearly takes care of Noah, bringing him safely to the other side.

2 God will judge the entire world in the future with a global conflagration on the Last Day.

Read Luke 17:26-30

"Just as it was in the days of Noah, so will it be in the days of the Son of Man. They were eating and drinking and marrying and being given in marriage, until the day when Noah entered the ark, and the flood came and destroyed them all. Likewise, just as it was in the days of Lot—they were eating and drinking, buying and selling, planting and building, but on the day when Lot went out from Sodom, fire and sulfur rained from heaven and destroyed them all—so will it be on the day when the Son of Man is revealed."

Why does Jesus go to the judgment of Noah's day as a point of comparison for the suddenness and extent of His return?

The global flood of Noah's day was a worldwide judgment that provided the pattern for Jesus' second coming. In that instance, there were no indicators that the judgment was impending, but people were going about their daily lives assuming all would continue as it had been. Note the repetitive phrase Jesus uses: *"and destroyed them all."* He wants people to be aware of the destruction that will come with His second coming.

Peter says *"that by means of these the world that then existed was deluged with water and perished."* When he talks about the fire of judgment, he says *"all these things are thus to be dissolved."* What are the differences between these two types of global judgments?

As Dr. Steve Boyd pointed out in the film, the global flood returned the earth to a water ball as it was in Genesis 1:2. In the future judgment, God will use fire to burn up the earth, then completely re-make it as the new heavens and earth.

3 The only salvation from the coming global judgment is through the grace of Jesus Christ.

Read 2 Peter 2:4-10

For if God did not spare angels when they sinned, but cast them into hell and committed them to chains of gloomy darkness to be kept until the judgment; if he did not spare the ancient world, but preserved Noah, a herald of righteousness, with seven others, when he brought a flood upon the world of the ungodly; if by turning the cities of Sodom and Gomorrah to ashes he condemned them to extinction, making them an example of what is going to happen to the ungodly; and if he rescued righteous Lot, greatly distressed by the sensual conduct of the wicked (for as that righteous man lived among them day after day, he was tormenting his righteous soul over their lawless deeds that he saw and heard); then the Lord knows how to rescue the godly from trials, and to keep the unrighteous under punishment until the day of judgment, and especially those who indulge in the lust of defiling passion and despise authority.

What is the comparison Peter is making in terms of how God will treat the godly versus the ungodly? Why is this an important distinction?

God's justice requires that He punish sinners for their sins. Peter says that this justice applies equally to angels, to those in Noah's day, to those in Sodom and Gomorrah, and to those living in the times of Peter up to our day. The comparison is between those who will be punished and those whom He preserves, such as Noah and Lot. Peter therefore wants his readers to take heart that God will also preserve them.

Why does it matter that God did not spare angels when they sinned?

If angels, who are greater and more powerful beings, were also judged and cast into hell, then we can sure those living in our generation who reject the Lord will also be judged.

God is always the one identified with saving Noah and Lot from the judgment inflicted on those around them; how does Jesus save us from *"the wrath to come?"* (Matthew 3:7)

Jesus provides salvation for us through His life of righteousness, death on the cross, and resurrection from the dead. These three things provide us His righteousness, His substitutionary death and atonement on our behalf, and His resurrection life that raises our spirits and bodies from the dead.

Closing Thoughts

The doctrine of the judgment of God is one of the most important doctrines in the Bible, yet it is also one of the most ignored in modern churches. The reality of the global judgment of the Flood is seen in the enormous layers of rock all around the earth. They should be a constant reminder to us that God judged the world in the past and therefore will judge it again in the future. Peter himself points to our only hope of salvation: *"This Jesus is the stone that was rejected by you, the builders, which has become the cornerstone. And there is salvation in no one else, for there is no other name under heaven given among men by which we must be saved."* (Acts 4:11-12)

A Local Flood

In the late 18th and early 19th centuries, a number of geologists began to argue that the thick sedimentary rock layers on the earth were not formed quickly during a global flood, but slowly over long ages. As a result of this shift in interpretation, a number of Christian pastors and theologians began to reinterpret verses referring to the Flood as a local, rather than a global, inundation.

That view has continued to this day. Many commentaries, study Bibles, and Bible encyclopedias incorporate this interpretation of a local flood into their publications. They often change the translation of the Hebrew word historically translated as "earth" to "land," then explain that Genesis 6-8 is referring to a local flood that only covered a section of Mesopotamia rather than the entire world.

Many Biblical commentators are convinced that conventional geologists cannot be wrong in their interpretation of the source of the rocks. At the same time, they realize the flood is written as a historical event in Genesis, and is referred to as a historical event in other parts of the Bible. Their solution is to re-interpret the Genesis flood as a local flood that occurred somewhere in the Middle East, thereby avoiding a direct conflict with the interpretations of conventional geologists.

Inevitably, this creates a new set of problems.

- Why was Noah told to save two of every kind of animal when they could easily have survived in other parts of the world?

- Why was a vessel as big as the ark needed?

- Why did God say He was going to destroy all flesh everywhere, when He really wasn't?

- Wouldn't people and animals just flee to an area of the world not affected by the local flood?

- If God promised not to flood the earth again, why do major local floods continue to occur all over the world?

- Why has the vocabulary used in Genesis always been interpreted to refer to a global flood up until the 18th century?

- Why do other people in the Bible (such as Peter and Jesus) refer to the Flood as a global event?

The interpretive problems of a local flood multiply as one tries to fit it into the historical narrative of the Bible.

Of course, from a geological perspective, things don't get any easier when one attempts to establish a massive, year-long flood in the Middle East large enough to inundate everything. In a personal conversation, sedimentary geologist Dr. Steve Austin pointed out that the sedimentary evidence for a flood large enough to float Noah's ark is not observable in the right places in Mesopotamian strata. Small floods have been identified in some archeological strata, but they are not large enough to float a boat as big as the Ark for a year. Furthermore, assuming the current configuration of the Mesopotamian basin, the water of even a major local flood would quickly flow into the Persian Gulf via the Tigris and Euphrates rivers.

In spite of these things, the desire to maintain some sort of concord with the conventionally-accepted scientific view is extremely powerful.

Yet many Christians do not realize how the flood relates to the doctrine of judgment. A global flood is obviously being held up by Jesus and Peter as the model of the coming global judgment of God—not only in extent, but in suddenness and complete destruction.

Why is one's view of the extent of the flood so important to the doctrine of judgment?

Everything goes back to what one thinks of the majority of the sedimentary rock layers on the earth. They are thick, they are enormous in extent, and they are filled with billions of dead creatures. If one sees them as the result of a global flood, then the text fits neatly with the world around us. The layers are therefore snapshots of different ecosystems existing before the Flood that *"had corrupted their way on the earth"* and which God wiped out in judgment.

This means there is a constant, visual reminder of God's judgment everywhere in the world. When one looks up and sees the massive layers of rock with endless fossils in them, one should think: 'That is what happened as a result of sin leading to judgment.' If one holds to a global flood, the doctrine of judgment is embedded into the very fabric of our world.

If, however, one sees the rock layers as the result of the slow rise and fall of epicontinental seas over hundreds of millions of years, then God's judgment is erased from the earth. The rock layers are not a picture of punishment for sin, but of deep time. They instead provide a record of hundreds of millions of years of corruption, disease, and death for countless creatures living long before Adam.

This presents an additional set of problems for Christians who hold to a local flood: how do you explain the fossils within the rock layers if God created all creatures fully-formed as distinct kinds?

One solution proposed by a French naturalist in the early 19th century was that different types of creatures were progressively created by God at various times in the past. When some died out during extinction events, God replaced them millions of years later with new creatures. This "progressive creation" process happened over and over again until, eventually, God created Adam and Eve.

A prerequisite for this view is that one must assume the record of creation in Genesis is allegorical; it certainly cannot be literal. There is no mention anywhere of multiple creation events of successive types of marine creatures, plants, birds, and animals separated by long periods of time. Furthermore, there's no clear connection between the actual events recorded in Genesis and what we see in the rock layers.

By the mid-19th century, progressive creation was becoming more and more difficult to defend. As a result, progressive creationists were eventually replaced by the next generation of evolutionary theorists.

This began with the publication of Charles Darwin's *The Origin of Species* in 1859. In the last chapter of his book in which he summaries his argument, it is obvious his true opponents are progressive creationists who assert that God created all the creatures on the earth at various times and in various places over long ages.

Darwin's ideas made quick work of progressive creation. Within a generation, most scientists and many theologians adopted evolutionary theory as the best explanation of how varieties of life came to be on the earth.

An argument could therefore be made that it was the rejection of a global flood by 18th- and 19th-century geologists and Christians that led to the eventual rejection of the entire doctrine of creation.

The issue, therefore, goes back to the rocks: are they the result of long ages and slow processes or a short period and global judgment?

The history of these issues should give pause to modern evangelical Bible scholars desiring to interpret Genesis 6-8 as a local flood. Not only does this reinterpretation transform the doctrine of judgment, but it opens the door for the rejection of other basic Biblical doctrines, starting first with the doctrine of creation.

If the first judgment of the world was not truly global, should anyone be worried about the coming judgment? This is the argument the Apostle Peter says "scoffers" were making in the first century. Curiously, it is not dissimilar to the arguments made today by agnostics and atheists.

If, however, one realizes the massive layers of rock that are filled with dead creatures are the result of a global flood, it transforms one's understanding of history. God's judgment suddenly becomes very real.

NOTE: We expand on this history in the next 'Differing Views: The Age of the Earth'

God judged the entire world in the past with the global flood of Noah's day.

Read 2 Peter 3:1-6

This is such an important passage for understanding God's judgment, it is worth reviewing in depth. Notice how the real argument between the scoffers and Peter concerns *history*. A dispute concerning what actually happened in the past bears on what will actually happen in the future.

- What is the future event that scoffers do not want to admit will happen?

- What are the prior events that scoffers want to overlook as having happened?

- Why are the historical facts of God's creation of the world and His global judgment with the flood so important when considering the future? Why are these related?

- Why do you think people want to overlook them?

- Peter talks about the world that then was being destroyed—what does this tell us about God's judgment?

- In his first letter, Peter draws a comparison between the waters of the flood and the water of baptism. (1 Peter 3:21) What is the point of comparison between them?

The creation and the Flood are essential to understanding where history is headed. It should not be surprising that many people want to overlook them.

Pray that the true history of the world would be made manifest in this generation.

God will judge the entire world in the future with a global conflagration on the Last Day.

Read 2 Peter 3:7-13

The historical facts that God created the world then judged it with a global flood are what Peter wants people to remember when telling them what God will do in the future. God's actions in time are always front and center to Peter. Consider the following questions:

* Why does Peter make a comparison between a thousand years and a day? If time is irrelevant to God, to whom is it relevant?

* Why does Peter say God is waiting thousands of years before judging the world?

* Why have scoffers chosen to misinterpret God's forbearance and lack of current action as proof He never acted in the past?

* Peter describes the future judgment very specifically. How will that judgment change the entire universe?

Almost all of us are subject to the view that the history we live in is 'uniform' and will never change. Peter wants to remind us that this is an inaccurate view of history. When we look at the world around us, we should constantly remember the doctrines of creation and judgment, knowing that, in the future, God will judge and re-create the heavens and the earth.

Pray that God would give you eyes to see the truth of His actions in history, in the past, in the present, and in the future.

The only salvation from the coming global judgment is through Jesus Christ.

Read Hebrews 9:27-28

The doctrine of judgment stands alongside the doctrine of salvation: Christ is returning to save those *"who are eagerly waiting for Him."* From the Old Testament prophets through the book of Revelation, the authors of the Bible teach that *"man is appointed to die once and then face judgment."* Unless Christ saves us from that judgment, we will be like those men and women outside the ark during the global flood: there was nowhere for them to flee.

Hebrews draws a parallel between the Sabbath rest of the seventh day and the eternal salvation found in Christ. In this case, the rest of God is a rest that we can also enter through Christ.

Read Hebrews 4:1-13

- Why were some of those Israelites who heard the message not able to enter God's rest? What did they not unite that message with?

- We learned in a prior lesson that the Sabbath was made for man. How does that relate to the author of Hebrews comparing the Sabbath to heaven?

- According to this passage, is it possible that there are some who will have heard the message (in other words, some who grew up in church) not entering God's rest?

- How are we to strive to enter that rest?

The primary message of the New Testament is that we are all in danger of the coming global judgment of God. Our only hope to avoid that judgment is to trust in Christ to save us from it. Once we have truly repented of our sins and asked Christ to save us from the coming wrath, we have moved from death to life.

If you are unsure of your salvation from the future judgment of God, ask Jesus Christ to wash away your sins and to save you from the wrath to come.

6

The Importance of History

The Doctrine of Providence

"With the Bible, you have this notion that there is providence, a purposeful plan by God himself that is then worked out across time in a linear, understandable, traceable fashion."

— GEORGE GRANT

Read Isaiah 44:24-26 and 46:8-10

Thus says the LORD, your Redeemer, who formed you from the womb: "I am the LORD, who made all things, who alone stretched out the heavens, who spread out the earth by myself, who frustrates the signs of liars and makes fools of diviners, who turns wise men back and makes their knowledge foolish, who confirms the word of his servant and fulfills the counsel of his messengers..."

"Remember this and stand firm, recall it to mind, you transgressors, remember the former things of old; for I am God, and there is no other; I am God, and there is none like me, declaring the end from the beginning and from ancient times things not yet done, saying, My counsel shall stand, and I will accomplish all my purpose..."

Ask Questions

- **Why does the Lord first identify Himself in terms of what He did at creation?** God is establishing His ultimate authority over history since He is the one who formed time and space, then filled it with His works. There have always been idolatrous men who have sought to replace the history of God's actions revealed to His prophets with a history of their own making.

- **What is the comparison God highlights in terms of two different views of His actions in history?** On one side are "diviners" and "wise men" who are presenting their knowledge about God's actions as wisdom, when it is actually lies and foolishness. On the other side are God's servants and messengers speaking His word that He will confirm.

Watch Video 6 — "The Importance of History"
Paul Nelson, PhD, Philosopher of Science

Ask Questions

- Explore the four primary points of comparison between the conventional paradigm of history and the Genesis paradigm of history:

    1. What is the difference in terms of duration of time?

    2. What is the difference in terms of cause?

    3. What is the difference in terms of sequence of events?

    4. What is the difference in terms of one's view of reality?

- How is meaning different in these two views?

- Why is a witness important to how we view history? Does the Bible provide us an accurate witness to history?

The Doctrine of Providence

Time is extremely important to God. Because He created time as part of the heavens and earth, He continues to control everything that happens within time. Every moment is a connected link in the single chain of universal history.

This is what the prophet Isaiah reveals to us: God links together His initial creative acts with His control of history. The doctrine associated with God's control of history is called providence.

What is *providence?*

Providence is God's work of upholding the existence of the universe while guiding history to His designated ends.

The recurring metaphor in the Bible used to describe God's control over people and events is 'the potter and the clay': God actively shapes history into the form He desires. As He tells Jeremiah: *"Behold, like the clay in the potter's hand, so are you in my hand, O house of Israel."* (Jeremiah 18:5)

Not only does God act in history, but He ensured His past actions were accurately recorded. He did this by revealing His actions to trusted messengers such as Moses, Samuel, Isaiah, and others who wrote them under the influence of the Holy Spirit.

God also interprets His actions so they will not be misunderstood. As a result of the Fall, man often struggles to understand (or intentionally overlooks) what God has said and done. Both Isaiah and Peter refer to this sinful desire to ignore God's words and actions.

This brings us back to the doctrine of revelation that we studied in the first lesson. In order for everyone to know what God has done, He clearly explains His actions by revealing them to His prophets.

The doctrine of revelation teaches that if God did not reveal His actions to us, it would be impossible for us to know them. As a result, the doctrine of providence is directly related to God's revelation of Himself.

Providence explains why the creation reveals God's invisible attributes: not only does He maintain its design, but He controls even the smallest details of its history. As Jesus points out, *"Are not two sparrows sold for a penny? And not one of them will fall to the ground apart from your Father. But even the hairs of your head are all numbered. Fear not, therefore; you are of more value than many sparrows."* (Matthew 10:29-31)

The doctrine of providence is essential to understanding God's involvement in history. As the Psalmist explains: *The LORD brings the counsel of the nations to nothing; he frustrates the plans of the peoples. The counsel of the LORD stands forever, the plans of his heart to all generations.* (Psalm 33:10-11)

There are three aspects to our understanding of the doctrine of providence:

1 Jesus Christ not only created the world, but He continually upholds every aspect of it by His power.

Read Hebrews 1:1-4

Long ago, at many times and in many ways, God spoke to our fathers by the prophets, but in these last days he has spoken to us by his Son, whom he appointed the heir of all things, through whom also he created the world. He is the radiance of the glory of God and the exact imprint of his nature, and he upholds the universe by the word of his power. After making purification for sins, he sat down at the right hand of the Majesty on high, having become as much superior to angels as the name he has inherited is more excellent than theirs.

Why is it necessary for the universe (Greek "all things") to be upheld by Jesus' power?

When we create something, we make it and set it aside to continue to exist and work on its own; we are not needed for things to continue to operate. This is because the things we make rely on God's sustaining power to continue existing and working. Yet something must be supporting the universe; it is not self-sustaining. The Bible tells us that God upholds the universe by His power. Jesus must continue to maintain its existence at every point and every moment in time, otherwise it would cease to exist.

If time and space are an essential aspect of "all things," and history is what happens in time and space, then what does that tell us about Jesus' role in history?

Jesus upholds every aspect of history, down to the smallest details. This complete control over history is often misunderstood by us because we are small, limited creatures. We can sometimes think of God in a detached sense: sitting on His throne looking down on us. But the Bible teaches that He knows all things because He oversees all events. This should both encourage us and be a spur to personal holiness.

If the conventional paradigm of earth history sees events as being essentially random, how is God's providence the opposite of that view?

Randomness ultimately has no direction to it; if it did, it would not be random. The doctrine of providence teaches that, ultimately, there is nothing random in the universe.

2 God created the earth for man to live on, then revealed His creative work in Scripture to ensure man knew what He had done.

Read Isaiah 45:11-12, 18-19

Thus says the LORD, the Holy One of Israel, and the one who formed him: "Ask me of things to come; will you command me concerning my children and the work of my hands? I made the earth and created man on it; it was my hands that stretched out the heavens, and I commanded all their host…"

For thus says the LORD, who created the heavens (he is God!), who formed the earth and made it (he established it; he did not create it empty, he formed it to be inhabited!): "I am the LORD, and there is no other. I did not speak in secret, in a land of darkness; I did not say to the offspring of Jacob, Seek me in vain.' I the LORD speak the truth; I declare what is right."

What does this passage tell us about God's purposes for creating the earth?

God created the earth to be inhabited by man. Everything we see around us, magnificent and amazing as it is, was all created for us so that we might have a place to seek the Lord and know Him.

How does God view the timing of His creation events, and the importance of that timing for His purposes?

God talks about creating the earth and placing man on it, of stretching out the heavens and all their host. He is reminding His listeners that all the events of creation happened at the same time because of His powerful word. When He speaks of these events in Isaiah, he is referring back to the events recorded in the first chapter of Genesis.

Why does God draw attention not just to what He *did*, but what He *said* about it?

God wants His people to know exactly what He has done in history because that is a source of trust for them. Furthermore, He wants them to know it has been intentional. The history recorded in Genesis is the foundation of how we know who God is. He wants His children to look to Him for answers concerning what has been and what will be. He is a mighty transcendent

God who also personally interacts with the people He has created. He always speaks what is right and true, and speaks in a way that man can understand.

The conventional view of history has a universe devoid of an earth for 9 billion years; it has a universe devoid of people for 13.8 billion years. Why is that view of time and history the opposite of what Isaiah tells us?

Isaiah says God created the earth for it to be inhabited by men: that was His purpose for creating it. Furthermore, He expressly says He did not create it empty. There is no suggestion of a slow, evolutionary, billions-of-years process in this passage; rather, it presents major, discontinuous events such as the creation of the earth, of man, and of the starry heavens. God then says He revealed the way He did it so that man would know and worship Him.

In the conventional view, however, there was no earth in the universe for the majority of its history. After it did slowly form, it took billions of years for it to evolve into something that could support life. In terms of human life, 99.9999% of the history of the universe is one of silent emptiness.

3 God has ordered when and where people live in time so that they will seek Him and repent before the coming Judgment.

Read Acts 17:22-34

So Paul, standing in the midst of the Areopagus, said: "Men of Athens, I perceive that in every way you are very religious. For as I passed along and observed the objects of your worship, I found also an altar with this inscription: 'To the unknown god.' What therefore you worship as unknown, this I proclaim to you. The God who made the world and everything in it, being Lord of heaven and earth, does not live in temples made by man, nor is he served by human hands, as though he needed anything, since he himself gives to all mankind life and breath and everything.

And he made from one man every nation of mankind to live on all the face of the earth, having determined allotted periods and the boundaries of their dwelling place, that they should seek God, and perhaps feel their way toward him and find him. Yet he is actually not far from each one of us, for "'In him we live and move and have our being'; as even some of your own poets have said, "'For we are indeed his offspring.'

Being then God's offspring, we ought not to think that the divine being is like gold or silver or stone, an image formed by the art and imagination of man. The times of ignorance God overlooked, but now he commands all people everywhere to repent, because he has fixed a day on which he will judge the world in righteousness by a man whom he has appointed; and of this he has given assurance to all by raising him from the dead."

How does Paul introduce God to the Athenians, and what does He say about Him?

He says that God made the world and everything in it, and is therefore Lord of heaven and earth.

Why is it important that we know that God gives life and breath and everything to mankind? What does this tell us about God's power and knowledge?

Paul is revealing that even the basic functions of our lives that we rely upon are in God's control. It tells us that God's power and knowledge are absolute.

What is Paul saying about Adam and his children in terms of God's control of their history? How is the choice of our birth at a certain time, in a certain place, to a certain family an enormous determiner of who we are?

We often don't consider how our lives are controlled by when and where we were born. A person born in China in 1240 to poor parents would live a radically different life than a person born in America in 1870 to middle class parents or to a person born in South Africa in 2000 to wealthy parents.

Why does God control our history?

God desires us to seek Him, know Him, and worship Him.

Paul begins by looking back in history, but ends by looking forward. What is the similarity between what he says in Acts 20 and what Peter says in 2 Peter 3 in terms of how we can know the future judgment is coming?

Paul says we know a future judgment is coming because God will judge the world through the man He has raised from the dead. Note that Paul does not even mention Jesus' name: the mere fact that he spoke of the resurrection caused people to speak out against him. These are similar to the scoffers that Peter refers to.

Closing Thoughts

The actions of God in history are essential to knowing who God is. The doctrine of providence teaches that God directs our steps in order for us to seek Him out and know Him. God's creation of the world and His complete control of history is for a purpose: to bring us to salvation through the work of His Son.

It is a great mystery to consider that Jesus created and upholds the world, and yet lived as a man, was crucified, and rose again for our salvation. This, however, is the mystery the authors of the New Testament teach, often being aware of its mysteriousness.

What they do not treat as mysterious is what God said happened in the past. God has clearly recorded what happened in Special Revelation: from creation in six days, to Adam and Eve formed in His image, to the universal effects of the Fall, to the Judgment of a global Flood, to Salvation in Jesus Christ.

The Bible is an accurate book of history that God expects us to know and trust. *For from him and through him and to him are all things. To him be glory forever. Amen.* (Romans 11:36)

The Age of the Earth

When we talk about the 'age' of something, we imply it has a specific history. For instance, if a man is ninety-five years old, he has lived through a series of events quite different from those of a ten-year-old boy.

Age indicates history.

This means when we talk about the age of the earth, we're really talking about the *history* of the earth. According to Genesis, it is a history that begins with specific events that lead eventually to Jesus Christ. In explaining this redemptive history, the prophet Isaiah is very clear: God controls every moment of time in order to glorify Himself by redeeming a people through the work of His Son. He says:

"I am God, and there is none like me, declaring the end from the beginning and from ancient times things not yet done, saying, 'My counsel shall stand, and I will accomplish all my purpose,'... I have spoken, and I will bring it to pass; I have purposed, and I will do it. Listen to me, you stubborn of heart, you who are far from righteousness: I bring near my righteousness; it is not far off, and my salvation will not delay; I will put salvation in Zion, for Israel my glory." (Isaiah 46:9-13)

God's providence ensures all of time and history serve His particular ends. Every moment is consequential and important because He is 'accomplishing all His purpose.' This is why the Bible is ultimately a book of history: it is through the events of real history that God brings salvation to us and glorifies Himself through it.

This is why one's view of the age of the earth matters to the gospel. If one replaces the Biblical timeline of thousands of years with the now-conventional timeline of billions of years, one must accept all the new events that go with that new timeline—events which necessarily displace Biblical events. This displacement inevitably affects the doctrines that rely on those events.

For example,

1. **God has accurately revealed the history of the universe** and man's role in it. To allegorize or de-historicize any of those historical events is to question the ability of special revelation to speak clearly about history.

2. **God created the entire universe fully-functional in six normal days.** To greatly extend the length of time and significantly alter events transforms the doctrine of creation into a slow, indirect, and death-filled process; this, in turn, transforms one's view of God and His nature.

3. **God formed Adam and Eve in His image at the beginning,** thereby ensuring His image would be reflected somewhere in the universe at every point in its history. If one places long ages before man's creation, it means God's image has been missing from creation for almost all of its history.

4. **God cursed the creation as a result of Adam's sin,** bringing death and corruption into a very good world. To say that there were billions of years of corruption and death before Adam's sin means God created a universe filled with death. This not only changes one's view of the fall, but of the nature of our redemption in time.

5. **God judged the entire world with a global flood,** killing all land creatures, birds, and people. The idea of a local flood not only violates the history revealed in special revelation, but it denies the past reality of global judgment in space and time, thereby casting doubt on the universality of the judgment to come.

6. **God providentially controls every moment of time and history,** starting with the first creation and the fall, guiding it to redemption in Christ, and ushering everything toward the new creation. If the timeline of the universe is not the timeline of the Bible, then God's providence is emptied of its meaning and purpose: it takes responsibility for billions of years of emptiness, silence, and death.

It is possible that many Christians do not realize how the age of the earth affects key doctrines related to the gospel. This has not always been the case. For most of the history of the church there was an understanding that one cannot change the history recorded in the Bible without changing the doctrines taught in the Bible.

Nevertheless, there are some Christians today who say the Bible does not even speak to the age of the earth. This view, however, would surprise the vast majority of interpreters throughout the history of the church.

Does the Bible speak to the age of the earth?

Starting in the first century AD and continuing to the present, most interpreters examined the genealogies in the Bible and said they can be used to calculate the age of the earth.

The first genealogy used this way is in Genesis 5. It reports that Adam fathered his son Seth at age 130, Seth fathered his son Enosh at age 105, and so on down to Noah who is said to have been 600 in the year of the Flood. If one sees Genesis 1 as a record of six normal days, and the genealogies as father-son relationships without gaps, then it appears one can calculate the time from Creation to the Flood.

The next genealogy using the same pattern is in Genesis 11. Noah's son Shem is said to have fathered Arpachshad two years after the Flood. The names and ages continue through Terah, the father of Abram, thereby providing a way to calculate the time between the Flood and Abraham's birth.

From Abraham forward, it is not as simple a process. There are no longer genealogies like the ones in Genesis 5 and 11 listing the father's age at his son's birth, so one must track down references to ages at significant events, cross-compare, then calculate together. This process takes one from Abraham to David; from David through the kings of Judah to the Exile; and from the Exile to Jesus' day.

Once this Biblical timeline is established, specific people and events are seen to intersect with other calendars in the ancient world. These can then be matched to an 'absolute' astronomical calendar to determine an approximate age for the earth. For instance, the Jewish historian Josephus, writing around AD 94, used this process to calculate the age of the earth as less than 6,000 years old.

For the moment, let's not worry about the critical views of the genealogies that emerged in the 19th century. Nor will we worry about the differing textual traditions, slight numerical variations, or questions concerning how dates are determined. The point is that prior to the 19th century, almost every significant Biblical commentator thought the Bible spoke to the age of the earth in a definitive way.[13]

---

13   Terry Morteson, *The Great Turning Point* (Master Books, 2012), 44-45.

So definitive, in fact, that specific numbers and ranges were regularly given. In the early church, these estimates were provided by Cyprian, Irenaeus, Clement of Alexander, Julius Africanus, Origen, Lactantius, Chrysostom, Jerome, and Augustine, all of whom put the age of the earth at less than 6,000 years from the date of their writing.

These systems of dating continued through the medieval church and persisted up to the 18th century with the well-known calculation of Archbishop Ussher (who preferred the Masoretic textual tradition to the Greek Septuagint used in the early church, thereby shrinking his timeline by over 1000 years). Ussher was actually just one of many Bible scholars who, although disagreeing on specifics, agreed that the age of the earth was less than 10,000 years old.

As was discussed in the last chapter, however, in the early 19th century the new sciences of geology and paleontology began to exert an influence on interpretations of Genesis.[14] James Hutton, George Cuvier, Charles Lyell, and others argued that the history of the earth was much older than 10,000 years; they based this view on their new interpretations of the rock layers and the fossils within them.[15] It became obvious that the traditional view and the new view could not both be accurate since they provided two competing histories of the earth.

This is an important observation: it was not simply a matter of differences in timescale, but of differences in events happening during those timescales. Everyone understood the implications of the profound change in age. In the new view of geology, the earth had a "deep history" with a series of events occurring in it that were radically different than the events recorded in special revelation.

Although non-Christians had already assigned Genesis to the realm of myth, these differences created a major issue for Christians: how did the history in Genesis fit with the new history of the earth? And what did it mean for the doctrines of revelation and creation?

---

14   Nigel M. de S. Cameron, *Evolution and the Authority of the Bible* (The Paternoster Press, 1983), 72.

15   Martin Rudwick, *Earth's Deep History* (The University of Chicago, 2014), 99, 110.

One option was to question the geological findings themselves. This was done by a series of "scriptural geologists" with limited success. Terry Mortenson documents this history in his book *The Great Turning Point*.

The other option was to change one's interpretation of Genesis.

As a result, the 19th century saw the introduction of a number of new interpretations that attempted to synthesize Genesis 1 with a much longer period of time.[16] One was the 'gap' view which argued there was an indefinitely long period of time between Genesis 1:1 and 1:2.

Another idea was the 'day-age' view which said each 'day' in Genesis 1 was actually a long period of time. There was much discussion as to just how long a period of time, as well as which events each 'day' symbolized, but in the end, this view provided a symbolic or allegorical function that could be shifted as needed to match changing scientific views.

The result of these interpretations was that, for those who held them, it no longer became possible to determine the age of the earth from the Bible. Instead, it was the role of geologists to determine the age of the earth. This meant that geologists became the new historians of the earth, removing from the Bible the ultimate authority concerning the actual history of creation.

Some commentators and pastors argued this was an incorrect way of interpreting Genesis 1; they said these new views were neither in the history of interpretation nor in the text itself. In spite of this, it became more and more popular to interpret Genesis in light of the seemingly indisputable claims of many geologists that the earth was far older than 10,000 years. For some, it was an easy concession because it seemed to maintain the historical integrity of Adam and Eve as well as the rest of the Biblical text.

The one nagging problem was the fossil record.

By this point, everyone knew there were fossilized remains of dead creatures and plants in the rocks, often in very specific layers and patterns. Although some of these creatures were clearly extinct (such as the dinosaurs), some looked very similar to species still living on the earth.

This raised an additional series of questions: If God created all these organisms, when did He do it? And how did they get into the rocks in such

---

16   Mortenson, 33, 35.

specific patterns? Furthermore, if they were examples of creatures that died long before Adam, how did their deaths fit with the doctrines of creation and the fall in terms of an originally good earth cursed with corruption?

Where do fossils fit into the Bible?

Let us return momentarily to the record of Biblical interpretation. From the first century onward, there was a nearly unanimous view that all living creatures in the world were created fully-formed as distinct "kinds" on creation days three, five, and six. These kinds could be seen in the various species that were then alive (allowing for some variation in how one defined 'species' and 'kind').

There was also agreement that living creatures were created "good" in a "very good" world. This meant harmony amongst living organisms and the absence of death in the world.[17]

Finally, there was an understanding that the flood of Noah's day covered the entire earth, killing all flying creatures and land animals. This meant that, up to the 18th century, when fossils of different creatures were found in the mountains of Europe, they were assumed to be the remains of creatures killed during Noah's flood.[18] The large layers of rock in which the fossils were found were therefore the result of God's global judgment.

By the late 18th century, however, geological views were changing concerning the source of the rocks. If the layers were actually evidence of long ages rather than a global judgment, what were the fossils evidence of?

This question was taken up by naturalist Georges Cuvier in France. As the director of the Museum of Natural History, he had amassed the largest collection of fossils in the world and was considered the foremost expert on extinct creatures—particularly their unique forms.[19]

Cuvier thought the extraordinary design of fossilized animals meant they had originally been created by God in the same form in which they had been buried. He looked at the different species found in successive layers of

---

17   Fr. Seraphim Rose, Genesis, *Creation, and Early Man* (St. Herman of Alaska Brotherhood, 2011), 705-7.

18   Mortenson., 43.

19   Edward J Larson, *Evolution* (Modern Library, 2004), 19.

rock and argued that God progressively created creatures at various times and places in the world, all separated by long ages and great distances.

These long ages ended with catastrophic extinction events in which large numbers of species died out. The catastrophes were followed by God starting over again creating many new species in different places all over the earth. This cyclical process occurred dozens of times until man was finally created in the most recent creation event.[20]

The fossils, in Cuvier's schema, were additional evidence of an old earth. This meant not only long ages before Adam, but ages filled with the violent death and extinction of countless species of God's creatures. For some, this was a history difficult to reconcile with the record in Genesis, even if Genesis was a symbolic record. Genesis said nothing about death and extinction; in fact, all prior interpretations had pointed to a paradise on earth.

What became of Noah's flood?

For a while, geologists saw evidence for the flood to the highest rock layers. But by the mid-19th century, even this data was reinterpreted as evidence for an ice age. The flood of Noah's day was finally determined to be a local flood, likely somewhere in Mesopotamia.

Numerous Biblical commentators responded in kind, adjusting their interpretations to make room for the new views of the flood. The doctrine of global judgment, which had always been associated with the great deluge, now became more of a symbolic judgment occurring in a localized area.

By this point, it was obvious that many of the doctrines held by Biblical interpreters for almost two millennia had been significantly altered. Nevertheless, although many concessions had been made to the new geological historians, some Christians thought that at least God's historic role in creating Adam, Eve, and all the living creatures had been retained.

It was not to last for long.

What does evolution mean for the Bible?

Progressive creation over long ages was the established view when Charles Darwin entered the scene. Unlike Cuvier and other geologists, however, Dar-

---

20   Larson, 24.

win had been convinced for decades that progressive creation could neither explain all the data nor fit with his agnosticism. Instead, he thought gradual evolution and change from simpler to more complex forms was a preferable explanation.

It was this theory he presented in 1859 in *The Origin of Species*. He opened his volume with a brief historical sketch of the various views on the subject up to his day. Knowing his opponents were progressive creationists, he quotes naturalist Thomas Huxley saying, "If we supposed that each species of animal and plant, or each great type of organisation, was formed and placed on the surface of the globe at long intervals by a distinct act of creative power;... it is well to recollect that such an assumption is as unsupported by tradition or revelation as it is opposed to the general analogy of nature."[21] In other words, progressive creation was not found in the history of ideas, nor in the Bible, nor in what we see in the world around us.

Darwin would go on to lay out his arguments against special creation. He first argued for the evolution of all living organisms from a single common ancestor in *Origin*, then added the evolution of humans in *The Descent of Man*. As he put it, "When I view all beings not as special creations, but as the lineal descendants of some few beings which lived long before the first bed of the Cambrian system was deposited, they seem to me to become ennobled."[22]

His arguments were so persuasive that a majority of scientists shifted their views from progressive creation to evolution within just a few decades.[23] As a result, Darwin and many others completely rejected God's role in the creation or formation of any living creature. They did not see evolution in any way compatible with the revelation in the Bible, nor with doctrines like creation and providence.[24]

In spite of this, some Christians like scientist Asa Gray introduced the concept of "theistic evolution" in an attempt to merge Christian doctrines with Darwin's history. Some Biblical interpreters then modified the day-age

---

21 Charles Darwin, *The Origin of Species* (The University of Chicago, 1989), 5.

22 Darwin, 243.

23 Larson, 107-8.

24 Charles Darwin, *Variation Under Domestication, Vol 2* (1868), 431-2.

interpretation to fit the new scientific views of evolution, including what it said about the natural history of the world.

This led to a few final questions: if neither living creatures nor man had been created by God instantly, then what was one to make of Adam and Eve? How could they be the original two humans if they both had mothers and fathers? Were they even real?

By this point, it seemed obvious to many that the first chapters of Genesis could only be accepted as theological symbolism and mythology, not actual history. Special revelation could not be trusted to provide an accurate history of the world.

Thomas Huxley summed it up well in 1890: "The books of ecclesiastical authority declare that certain events happened in a certain fashion; the books of scientific authority say they did not."[25]

Over the space of a hundred years, what started as an adjustment in age ended with a completely new history of the earth, its living creatures, and man himself.

It was inevitable that a change in history would be reflected by a change in doctrine. One need only follow the rise of liberal theology in the 19th and early 20th centuries to see the results of that change. Although that history includes additional lines of influence, the impact of the then-new scientific history of the world cannot be underestimated.

It is not surprising that the doctrines examined in this study were all discarded at various times on the path to the 20th century: revelation, creation, the image of God, the fall, judgment, and providence came to be considered by many churches as 'primitive' ideas that had some use in helping us live our lives, but were not connected to anything real.

The age of the earth had changed; so must the doctrines that were connected to that age.

The age of the earth and Christian doctrine

Today, this connection is lost on many Christians. It was lost on many intelligent men of the 19th century, most of whom did not realize how their succes-

---

25   Cameron, 82.

sive compromises ended up sacrificing the doctrinal foundation of the gospel.

There still remain Christians who follow a form of Cuvier's 'progressive creation' or a form of Asa Gray's 'theistic evolution.' It is logical therefore that both groups must sacrifice basic Christian doctrines in order to maintain these views. These Christians reside in a middle ground between the Biblical view of history and the conventional view. They borrow from both, but are consistent with neither.

Nigel Cameron accurately sums it up: "Men like S.R. Driver...made very clear what the choice actually is: between accepting the Genesis narratives in an essentially 'literal' sense—as teaching what they plainly intend to teach— and rejecting them as teaching anything about the origin of the world. The middle ground, which evangelicals then as now desired to occupy, is untenable."[26]

Why is it untenable?

Because the integrity of essential Christian doctrines rest on the Biblical view of events as presented in Genesis. Even though many Christians who occupy the middle ground are well-meaning, they cannot provide a positive structure of natural history that fits with the written record, not only in Genesis, but throughout the rest of the Bible.

The history of the 19th and 20th centuries does not bode well for purveyors of these views. The children of progressive creationists inevitably become theistic evolutionists, and their children eventually become atheistic evolutionists. This is a historic pattern. When one generation begins questioning the historical accuracy of some parts of the Bible, the next generation takes this questioning to its logical conclusions. The history of Western Europe and America is very clear here: why should one believe in something that didn't really happen?

It is a dangerous course when Christians start questioning historical events that form the foundation of their faith. Those who seek to replace the Biblical age of the earth with the conventional age are simply replacing Biblical history with a history intended to make the resurrection of Jesus impossible.

Of course Paul understood this. It is why questions about the history of

---

26   Cameron, 83.

the earth are of central importance to him. As he reminds us, it is only when we start with the history recorded in Genesis as true history that we can begin to understand the true nature of our salvation:

"Now if Christ is proclaimed as raised from the dead, how can some of you say that there is no resurrection of the dead? But if there is no resurrection of the dead, then not even Christ has been raised. And if Christ has not been raised, then our preaching is in vain and your faith is in vain. We are even found to be misrepresenting God, because we testified about God that he raised Christ, whom he did not raise if it is true that the dead are not raised. For if the dead are not raised, not even Christ has been raised. And if Christ has not been raised, your faith is futile and you are still in your sins. Then those also who have fallen asleep in Christ have perished. If in Christ we have hope in this life only, we are of all people most to be pitied.

"But in fact Christ has been raised from the dead, the firstfruits of those who have fallen asleep. For as by a man came death, by a man has come also the resurrection of the dead. For as in Adam all die, so also in Christ shall all be made alive. But each in his own order: Christ the firstfruits, then at his coming those who belong to Christ. Then comes the end, when he delivers the kingdom to God the Father after destroying every rule and every authority and power. For he must reign until he has put all his enemies under his feet. The last enemy to be destroyed is death. For 'God has put all things in subjection under his feet.' But when it says, 'all things are put in subjection,' it is plain that he is excepted who put all things in subjection under him. When all things are subjected to him, then the Son himself will also be subjected to him who put all things in subjection under him, that God may be all in all." (1 Corinthians 15:12-28)

Jesus Christ not only created the world, but He continually upholds every aspect of it by His power.

Read Colossians 1:15-23

This section of Paul's letter to the Colossians is one of the more theological-ly-dense sections of all his letters. Paul opens his epistle by linking together different aspects of Christ's nature and works, starting with His involvement in creation, moving to His work on the cross, and ending with His gift of faith and salvation to the letter's readers. There is a lot in this passage, so it is worth reading multiple times to take in what he is saying.

- How does the doctrine of providence run through the entire passage? Consider the steps of Paul's historical approach to explaining Christ's work.

- How does the doctrine of the image of God relate to this passage? Why is it important that Jesus is the image of the invisible God? Since Jesus precedes Adam, what does that suggest about whose image Adam is made in?

- How does the doctrine of creation relate to what Paul explains about Jesus and His central role in creation?

- Although difficult to comprehend, why is it important to know that in Christ *"all things hold together?"*

- If the doctrine of the Fall says there was a universal disruption due to Adam's sin, why is it important that Christ *"reconcile to himself all things, whether on earth or in heaven…making peace by the blood of the cross?"*

- How is our personal reconciliation with God to make us *"holy and blameless"* a part of the universal reconciliation, in which Jesus is returning the world to its original state of righteousness?

Although there is much in this passage that is difficult to understand, it is clear that Jesus occupies the central role of the universe from the very beginning of creation to the very end of time. Moreover, our individual salvation and faith is an important part of that enduring history.

Pray that God would open your eyes to see how your salvation is part of a universal renewal of the entire heavens and earth.

God created the earth for man to live on, then revealed His creative work in Scripture to ensure man knew what He had done.

Read Psalm 104

This is the great psalm of praise to God for what He has done in the creation. It is an example of how poetic language refers to historical events recorded in other parts of the Bible. Poetry is not *ahistorical* language; rather, it dramatizes and colors the actual events of history.

In this case, it is the first chapters of Genesis that are in view alongside the world of the psalmist's day.

- Why is it important that the psalmist first brings up the role of light?

- How does the psalmist use the metaphor of the tabernacle (a tent) in the first section?

- To what part of the Genesis history do verses 5 to 9 refer? Note that *"the waters stood above the mountains," "the mountains rose, the valley's sank down,"* and a boundary was set so that the waters *"might not again cover the earth."* Where is this recorded in Genesis?

- How is the doctrine of providence revealed in God's continual taking care of animals and plants?

- How do verses 14-15 explain how God provides for man's every need?

- What day of creation do verses 19-23 explore, and how does it relate to that day of creation?

- What does verse 23 tell us about the importance of how God set up our solar cycle to provide a daily schedule for man's work?

- How do verses 24-30 explain about the God's ongoing role in regard to living creatures?

- What do verses 31-35 tell us about our appropriate response to God when considering what He has done to create the world and continues to do to sustain it?

- Explain how the psalmist sees the current world where men make wine, ships sail on the sea, and animals hunt for food in light of the original world created by God? How is God's providence the connection between them?

Poetic language is an important way the authors of the Bible talk about God's actions in time. Because these actions are so extraordinary, poetry is one of the best ways to understand their power, magnificence, and beauty. But poetry only makes sense if it is referring to actual historical events.

Pray that God would give you language to worship Him for the amazing things He has done.

God has ordered when and where people live in time so that they will seek Him and repent before the coming Judgment.

Read Isaiah 40

This is one of the greatest prophetic chapters in the entire Old Testament, quoted often by the authors of the New Testament. The prophet Isaiah looks to the future, seeing the preaching of John the Baptist, the impending Judgment, and the coming of Jesus Christ who will *"tend his flock like a shepherd."*

After this first section, Isaiah turns his eyes up to God to announce His majesty as Creator.

- What do verses 12-17 teach us about the power and majesty of God? How is the doctrine of creation assumed in the passage?

- Why does Isaiah refer back to *"the beginning"* and *"the foundations of the earth"* to make his point?

- What do verses 23 and 24 tell us about how God orders people lives?

- The people of Judah and Israel were concerned that God was ignoring them or had forgotten them. What does Isaiah say in response to this?

- Why is it amazing to consider that the God who created the heavens and the earth also watches over the basic needs of His people? How does this last section relate to what Isaiah says about Christ in verse 11?

The doctrine of providence should be a source of hope and encouragement for all those who put their trust in God. It teaches that the mighty God of the universe who created the heavens and the earth is also interested in the personal details of His people, taking care of their every need. It is *because* God created everything and controls everything that we can be sure that he will take care of everything and control everything in our own lives.

Pray that God would give you the perspective of Isaiah to see how He providentially controls everything.

About the Author

Thomas Purifoy Jr. is the producer, director, and writer of *Is Genesis History?* He decided to make a documentary on Genesis after a conversation with his then 10-year-old daughter about Creation and evolution. After graduating from Vanderbilt University in 1994, he served four years as an officer in the U.S. Navy. He has directed a classical school in France where he taught literature, philosophy, history, Bible, and filmmaking.

Thomas currently works as a producer with Compass Cinema (CompassCinema.com). He also creates and sells homeschool curriculum through Compass Classroom (CompassClassroom.com). When he is not reading books, he is listening to classical music or watching old movies. He lives in Nashville, Tennessee with his wife and three daughters.

Beyond
IS GENESIS HISTORY?

If you want to **dig deeper into the science and scholarship** behind the feature documentary, seek out these additional volumes.

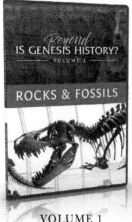

VOLUME 1
Rocks & Fossils
Now Available

VOLUME 2
Life & Design
Spring 2018

VOLUME 3
Bible & Stars
Spring 2018

Available at
IsGenesisHistory.com

"You are the Lord, you alone. You have made heaven, the heaven of heavens, with all their host, the earth and all that is on it, the seas and all that is in them; and you preserve all of them; and the host of heaven worships you."

—Nehemiah 9:6